ACADEMIA LUNARE
Call For Papers 2017

The Evolution of African Fantasy and Science Fiction

Edited By
Francesca T Barbini

Editor Foreword © Francesca T Barbini 2018
Articles © is with each individual author 2018
A portion of Polina Levontin's article has appeared in 'Scientists in Nigerian/Western Science Fiction' published in *Foundation: The International Review of Science Fiction*, Spring 2018.

First published by Luna Press Publishing 2018

The Evolution of African Fantasy and Science Fiction © 2018. All rights reserved. No part of this publication may be reproduced, stored in a retrieval system, or transmitted in any form or by any means, electronic, mechanical, photocopy, recording or otherwise, without prior written permission of the copyright owners. Nor can it be circulated in any form of binding or cover other than that in which it is published and without similar condition including this condition being imposed on a subsequent purchaser.

www.lunapresspublishing.com

ISBN-13: 978-1-911143-51-2

Contents

On the Emergence of African Science Fiction
Peter J. Maurits   1

Forces Shaping the Development of South African speculative fiction down the ages
Nick Wood   29

The Dangers of Expectation in African Speculative Fiction
Ezeiyoke Chukwunonso   51

Scientists in Nigerian Science Fiction
Polina Levontin   71

Portrayals of South Africans in Popular Entertainment: Bad Accented Baddies, Prawns and Black Panther
Robert S. Malan   97

Biographies   110

On the Emergence of African Science Fiction

By Peter J. Maurits[1]

The aim of this article is to contribute to the understanding of the emergence of contemporary science fiction on the African continent (ASF), occurring around the year 2007. Based in part on theories of the emergence of European and American SF, I suggest that we may consider ASF a new phase in the joint tradition of science fiction and utopian writing that responds to both contemporary and non-contemporary narrative dystopian traditions. I suggest that ASF could build and maintain momentum due to the spread of new media on the African continent, due to Afro- and techno-optimism, and the effects of the global financial crisis (GFC) on discursive regimes connected to the narrative utopia.

When the number of African science fiction publications increased during the 2000s, a heated debate on the origin of the genre occurred alongside it. Centring on the seemingly neutral question of, "is African science fiction (ASF) a new, old, local or alien cultural form?", the very nature of what African cultural production should or could be was perceived to be at stake. Dilman Dila summarises this well in his blogpost "Is Science Fiction Really Alien to Africa?" (2015). "African writers", he says, "forever have to defend their work." They are expected to write about the "problems of their societies", and when they do, "someone wonder[s] why they only write about misery and gloom on the continent". When they write

---

1. I am grateful to Thomas Erthel, Hrvoje Tutek, Dani Bodor, and my colleagues at the American department of the University of Erlangen-Nuremberg for their comments.

science fiction they are called "'copycat'", or worse, are told that Africans are unable to "write such stories". Clearly, as Dila implies, there is no reason to claim that writers' geographical locations more or less entitle or enable them to use a genre, especially because the contemporary literary system is a "world-literary system" (Moretti, 2000:56). That term connotes the movement of literary (but also cinematographic) forms over the entire globe (on unequal terms) and the formation of new forms resulting from the convergence of traveling form and local content. Dila describes this process relative to the formation of contemporary ASF, when he indicates that, while some stories draw on "popular Western films and books", they also draw on local "folk tales", and so on (2015).

Dila continues to discuss some common misconceptions, and the importance of ASF writers' position in the world-literary system, making his account, arguably, one of the more valuable contributions to the debate. Nevertheless, while Dila pursues the 'is ASF new' question, I want to suggest displacing it and the normativity associated with it altogether. In my understanding, cultural forms are a function, or are symptomatic, of their historical context, roughly meaning that (in this case) a genre emerges for specific historical reasons. It would follow that the presence or absence of a specific cultural form is not a qualitative indicator of a (or part of a) cultural system—as is implied in the debate—but rather an effect of a context of production. More importantly, it follows that to better comprehend the ASF phenomenon, the question of "is ASF new?" loses importance to that of "what are the historical reasons for ASF's emergence?", which is the main question of this essay.

To answer this question, ASF's emergence date must be

determined. I suggest doing so based on the sudden increase in the number of (known) publications that could be considered ASF. Based on several attempts to list ASF narratives,[2] it appears that there were about 10 ASF publications between 1900 and 1950, about 9 in the next 30 years, around 5 in the 1980s, and 5 in the 1990s. Then, there seems to have been 4 in 2007, 5 in 2008, 6 in 2009, and hundreds from 2010 onwards. This allows for determining more precisely the moment of what Geoff Ryman calls ASF's "lift-off" (2017: 2)—what I call emergence. That term, then, which I broadly understand following Raymond Williams (1977), does not refer to the publication of individual narratives, but to the start of a consistent and continent-wide increase in the number of ASF publications over an extended period. Based on these numbers, it appears that this increase occurred *around* 2007.[3]

Such periodisation allows us to move on to our question of why ASF emerged. In particular, I am interested in examining how theories of emergence of European and American SF (ESF, AmSF) may inform our understanding of ASF's emergence. As it is likely that this perspective is not exhaustive, my aim

---

2. I am indebted to the work of Mark Bould, Geoff Ryman, Wole Talabi, and Nick Wood, on which I draw here in part.

3. For Ryman, the lift-off started in the early 2000s, pointing to the impreciseness of 2007 as the year of emergence of ASF. Other factors contribute to this impreciseness: The ASF corpus can be defined differently. Ryman, for example, looks at *speculative fiction*, an umbrella term encompassing fantasy and horror. I look at SF only because there is reason to believe that, if the term fantasy applies to African literature, its history differs from that of ASF. Similarly, the specifier "African" may be defined differently, modifying what is included in the ASF corpus. For now, I broadly follow Bould (2015) in considering "African" a heterogeneous and flexible category, which includes those who live on the African continent and those who self-identify as African. Even if a consensus on definitions could be reached, these numbers are problematic because it is likely that some ASF narratives are lost in what Margaret Cohen called *the great unread* (1999:23) and may never be found. Nevertheless, these numbers may be understood as providing an impression of ASF's emergence.

is adding to the existing literature rather than providing a complete account. In brief, I will suggest that ASF can be considered a new phase in the joint tradition of science fiction and utopian writing, responding to both contemporary and non-contemporary narrative dystopian traditions, and could build and maintain momentum due to the spread of *new media* on the African continent, due to techno-optimism, and the effects of the global financial crisis (GFC) on discursive regimes connected to the narrative utopia (section 3–5). In order to do so, I will first elaborate on some theories about the emergence of ESF/AmSF (section 1), and about why ASF did not emerge alongside ESF (section 2).

1. The emergence of ESF and AmSF

There "is really no good reason to expect that a workable definition of SF will ever be established", write Clute and Nicholls (1993:314). Partly, this is due to the lack of consensus on when the genre emerged. Literary historians can be roughly divided into those who support a long or short history. The first traces the genre back to classical antiquity, or the Copernican and Protestant revolutions. The second claims that sci-fi is a modern phenomenon, starting with *inter alia* Mary Shelley, Wells, or 1920s American pulp magazines.

Adam Roberts, supporting the long SF history, says that "the core of the [SF] genre" is formed by "stories of journeying through space" and time, of imaginary technology, and of narrative utopias (2006:vii-viii)—a broad but common SF understanding that I follow in this essay. Utopian narratives would not emerge until the 16th century, time travel narratives not until the 18th century, but journeys through space, including those involving imaginary technology, go back as far as what Roberts, using Verne's term, calls the Hellenistic, and later, Roman "*voyages extraordinaire*" (viii). Unlike in modernity, he says, ancient Hellenistic/Roman cosmology did not distinguish between "sky" and "outer space", but between the sky and the divine heavens instead (23). Hence, for the Greeks and Romans, voyages to the clouds and moon inhabit the same conceptual space and can both be considered (proto-) science fiction.

These early travel narratives are generally considered to be imaginary extrapolations of technological possibilities and *lived experiences* of societies in which sea travel "pervaded every aspect of life", including "commerce, politics, food production, cultural exchange, religion, and technological progress" (Beaulieu, 2016:24). They include, says Roberts, Aristophanes' play *Birds* (414 BC), Cicero's tale *The Dream of Scipio* (51 BC), and Lucian's *A True History* (176 AD)—in which the sky/moon provides a vantage point for judging society—and Plutarch's *The Moon* (80 AD), in which characters speculate about the contemporary scientific notions that the moon is made of a reflective earthly or fiery substance.

After these narratives, Roberts says, a large SF gap follows due to the dominance of Catholic cosmology in the medieval period: Humankind is the only form of intelligent material life and the Earth is the centre around which other celestial bodies move. This view was challenged during the Copernican revolution. It was proven that the Sun is the centre of our Solar System, decentring Earth and human existence, and "open[ing] the cosmos as a material space, available to imaginative explorations and colonization". This included "encounter[s] with alienness", which were previously unimaginable (2006:40). When heliocentrism had spread alongside the Protestant Reformation, a number of space-voyage narratives were produced, including the moon-voyage narratives by the British writers Francis Godwin (1638) and John Wilkins (1638), and the French writer Cyrano de Bergerac (1656).

Brian Aldiss, supporting a short history, says SF only started with Shelley's *Frankenstein* (1818), and followed the technological developments of modernity, including the invention and implementation of electricity, and Darwin's evolution theory. *Frankenstein*, he says, was "the first novel to be powered by evolution", and could open up the space to imagine the alien and, later, the cyborg (1973:26). Considering *Frankenstein*'s connection to the gothic genre, Aldiss had to argue that SF did not emerge from narrative voyages, but from the gothic genre instead, of which the supernatural elements were exchanged for technological and scientific ones.

For Roger Luckhurst it makes "little sense to talk about science fiction before 1880" (2005:16). He recognises the importance of technological, scientific, and evolutionary knowledge for SF, and calls SF the literature of a "technologically saturated society" (3). However, he continues to say that SF's "conditions of emergence" only came into being after *Frankenstein*. They included a literate working class, resulting from the 1870 Education act, availability of affordable reading materials (magazines), and a lived experience affected by technology (29). For Luckhurst, there is "no better embodiment of the conditions of emergence […] than Wells" (30).

Luckhurst also points to colonialism's importance for SF, an issue more comprehensively discussed by John Rieder (2012).

SF and colonialism, says Rieder, emerged in parallel. And the technological developments (e.g. marine engineering), and (evolutionary) science, and anthropology considered crucial to SF's emergence are "profoundly intertwined with colonial ideology and history" (2). The former constructed *inter alia* the *condition of possibility* of colonialism—mobility and military dominance. The latter two allowed colonisers to justify claims that newly encountered people and colonised subjects were inferior "savages", based on what were considered evolutionary and anthropological scientific grounds (4). For Rieder then, "the history, ideology, and discourses of colonialism" form part of SF's structure of feeling (33).

Samuel Delany, finally, argues that all these genealogies are "ahistorical" and "pedagogic snobbery (or insecurity)" (2011:25–6). For Delany, there is "no reason to run SF too much back before 1926, when Hugo Gernsback coined the ugly and ponderous term, 'scientifiction,' which, in the letter columns written by the readers of his magazines, became over the next year or so 'science fiction' and finally 'SF'" (26).

2. Why didn't ASF emerge alongside SF?

Based on the literary histories above, it could be suggested that the emergence of ESF and AmSF are related to imperial (maritime) "exploration" (Hellenistic period/colonisation), changes in belief systems (Catholicism vs Protestantism), scientific/technological developments (e.g. electricity, evolution theory, anthropology), material conditions (literacy, publishing), and the coinage of a term. And while they together echo the way in which the history of a so-called "Western Civilisation" is frequently narrated—neatly starting in Greece, continuing via Rome, France and England to the USA—a type of genealogy now widely considered Eurocentric, it may nevertheless provide a perspective from which to start determining why ESF, AmSF, and ASF did not emerge simultaneously. Without wanting to provide an exhaustive list, I will address what three of those reasons for non-emergence may be.

First, 17th century Europe. While the Copernican revolution and Protestant Reformation affected the African continent in a number of direct and indirect ways, Catholic dominance did not exist in Africa as in Europe during that time (Koschorke et al., 2007). Hence, the understanding of the cosmos did not change in the same way.

Second, publishing. As Nick Wood, among others, indicates, publishing ASF was "low in the priorities of local publishing houses" due to what editors perceived as an insufficient "black readership". This, he suggests, results from a "legacy of apartheid" in which "the 'white' and 'black' populations" did not get equal access to literacy (2009). While it is uncertain if this editorial perspective refers to an actual existing lack of readership, Wood's comment may be generalised from a historical perspective to a limited degree. Colonisers generally allowed only small groups of colonial subjects to learn how to read and write, in the hope that they would later govern the illiterate colonised in service of the coloniser. In some cases, this could have delayed the development of vast literary infrastructures as compared to some European countries. Hence, based on Luckhurst's conditions of possibility, it could be suggested that SF could not have emerged in some African countries with the same force as it did in, for example, the U.K., not even in the 1920s, because those conditions were insufficiently developed. Rachel Zadok, further, points to "risk-averse" publishers, who demand cultural forms from African writers that have been proven to sell, which did not include SF (cited in Dorman, 2015:1).

Third, colonisation. If SF relates to imperial or colonial (maritime) exploration, or as Rieder suggests, to the *structure of feeling* of a colonising society, it would not be unlikely that in societies subject to colonisation, other cultural forms than SF would have emerged instead. Notably, this SF-colonialism connection persists long after the large-scale decolonisation that started around 1960. Illustrative are Kubrick's *2001: A Space Odyssey* (1968) and Luc Besson's *The Fifth Element* (1997), which, respectively, reproduce the tropes of Africa as mankind's savage origin and of the exotic oriental in their opening scenes. In both cases, we see these areas (Africa/the "Orient") through the *colonial gaze*. Illustrative, too, is the Star Trek franchise. The film *Beyond* (2016) and the series *Discovery* (2017) revive the colonial trope of the savage cannibal vs. the civilised explorer (Krall/Klingons vs. Starfleet). And throughout the franchise, members of Starfleet recurrently attempt to separate the identities of explorer, scientist, and military personnel. Based on the above, it is unsurprising that these attempts are unsuccessful; like colonial exploration, Starfleet exploration entails science and military force. Consequently, variations of the phrase "Starfleet is about peaceful exploration" must be uttered recurrently to keep the idea of this separation intact. In short, SF still struggles to disconnect from its colonial history. This may also clarify Tchidi Chikere's impression that SF does not connect to the lived experience of Africans, and "will come [...] when it is relevant. [...] [N]ow, Africans are bothered about food, roads, electricity, water wars, famine, etc." (cited in Okorafor, 2014).

3. Why did ASF emerge around 2007?

Several possible causes for ASF's emergence may be extrapolated from the above, of which I address three. First, publishing. In the 2000s, an increase in mobile-phone ownership occurred on the African continent (as in many other places), and more inhabitants of the African continent have mobile phones (and internet access) now than landlines before. This trend is understood to be possible in part because mobile phones do not depend on a continuous connection to a power source and the infrastructure it involves (Kiregyera, 2015). Importantly, Ryman showed that ASF "happened" on "smartphones" (2017: 191). Narratives were initially circulated and consumed on blogs, websites, and webzines (e.g. *WordPress* and *Omenana*), which were often accessed using mobile phone technology. If this is so, mobile phone technology may be considered part of ASF's condition of possibility and adds to the saturation of society with technology. Proving an online success, "risk-averse" publishers and distributors could become more inclined to publish ASF.

Second, colonialism. Colonialism, in its 19th century form, has mostly ended, but SF's ties to it have not been severed. This may explain why ASF-exploration narratives are uncommon. Questions about ASF's relation to decolonisation remain open (can ASF be understood as facilitated by a form of decolonisation of SF? Can it be considered the decolonisation of SF? Etc.). Nevertheless, I will assume for now that the temporal distance to colonialism, and SF's internal heterogeneity (including narratives of journeys through space and time, imaginary technology, and narrative utopias), allow for expressing a variety of other concerns. This includes the "water wars" that Chikere mentions (cited in Okorafor, 2014), for instance, in the form of environmental post-apocalyptic ASF. Wanuri Kahiu's *Pumzi* (2009) also belongs to this category. Climate-change related social anxieties, in fact, appear frequently in ASF, and the sole reason that I do not list this as reason for emergence is that there is seldom a specific *cli-fi*-narrative structure. Instead, these concerns are incorporated thematically (e.g. sustainable-energy), or are interweaved in existing SF-narrative structures, as *Pumzi* also shows.

The most prominent narrative structure of ASF's emergence, which climate change concerns frequently latch onto is, arguably, a utopian one, or a *seemingly dystopian narrative utopia* (henceforth *D to U*). Roughly, the plots of these narratives depart from existing oppressive social structures that are subsequently challenged and/or overthrown by revolutions, creating the possibility of a better social system. Some examples: In *Pumzi*, the protagonist revolts against her oppressive government in order to plant a tree in what is claimed to be infertile wasteland; in Ahmed Khaled Towfik's *Utopia* (2009) the poor "Others" rebel to overthrow the parasitic rich; in Efe Okogu's "Proposition 23" (2012) the poor "undesirables" rise to overthrow the rich "citizens"; in Afolabi Muheez Ashiru's "Amphibian Attack" (2013) citizens overthrow rich oppressive businessmen; in Deji Olukotun's *Nigerians in Space* (2014) the militaristic government is defied to create the possibility of a technological revolution; in Boualem Sansal's *2084. The End of the World* (2015) the totalitarian regime's myths, essential for maintaining its dominance, are undermined; in Nick Wood's *Azanian Bridges* (2016), resistance against an Apartheid regime is organised; and so on.

The prominence of *D to U* points to a third possible reason for ASF's emergence. In order to specify this, a closer look at the narrative dystopia/anti-utopia, and at the narrative utopia, is necessary, and particularly, at the way in which these forms can be considered to be in competition with each other.[4] The anti-utopian narrative is thought to have first emerged around 1826; a reaction against US American utopian narratives/thought, intended to show the perceived dangers of utopianism (cf. Sargent, 1976:278). This notion—utopianism is dangerous—became generally accepted in the USA after the 1917 October Revolution and later during the Cold War, and a prominent if not dominant discourse emerged in most capitalist countries in which "utopia = totalitarianism = communism" (Levitas, 2007:297). In line with this, SF became predominantly anti-utopian. Utopian SF forms briefly re-emerged in the 1960s alongside the civil rights, anti-colonial, and anti-Soviet struggles, but lost momentum after the disappointment of the failure of 1968 (cf. Istvan Csicsery-Ronay, Jr., 2003). Anti-utopianism, including the narrative anti-utopia, re-established dominance after neoliberalism replaced Keynesianism as the new capitalist orthodoxy from roughly 1970 onwards. This could occur in part because neoliberalism and the narrative anti-utopia are able to mutually reinforce each other: A way for neoliberalism to be reproduced as the dominant political-economic creed, to create a consensus for that dominance

---

4. I will use the terms dystopia and anti-utopia interchangeably in this essay, although they are not the same, because they can both be considered to be in competition with the narrative utopia.

and, as such (discursively), eliminate competition of other systems, is via the creation of a discourse in which it is claimed that it is the only possible system, that there is no alternative (TINA). This was the original function of the narrative anti-utopia. Perry Anderson observes that, due to this anti-utopian spirit of the age, the narrative utopia "has been in general suspension since the mid-70s" (2004:71). Any utopian residue is "massively outweighed" by dystopian and anti-utopian forms (73).

In light of this brief history of (anti-)utopianism, ASF's *D to U* stands out in its historical moment—although it should be noted that the *topos* of revolution has seen numerous expressions in Hollywood productions of the last ten years or so too; an issue I will address on a different occasion. Notably, also in ASF's case, utopianism is evident in ASF narratives and the discourse that surrounds it—interviews, analyses, etc. *Omenana* editor Chinelo Onwualo makes a similar observation of an "emerging optimism" in her "work as a writer and editor of African science fiction" (2016:18). Roughly, this optimism draws on the presumed effects ASF may have on extra-textual reality, often in relation to technology: According to Raime Gbadamosi, ASF is connected to "the possibility of another future" (cited in Zvomuya, 2015:8) and, according to Nnedi Okorafor, SF in general "carries the potential to change the world" (2014:2), as it *inter alia* imagines possibly democratising technology. On the other hand, ASF optimism is connected to the perception of the African continent and its economy as strengthening. Arigbabu sees a connection between ASF's rise and "the shift in the economic center from the west" (2013:xii). Ryman comments that "this wave of creativity reminds [him] of Elizabethan England at the time of Shakespeare – the power is rising, and the literature with it" (2017). According to Wood, "it seems [that] the (diverse) African giant awakes – not just economically – but to the possibilities inherent in SF. Africa steadily appears to be becoming a more 'Hopeful Continent'" (2012:12).

Taking into account the importance of neoliberalism to the narrative (anti-)utopia, as well as the perceived state of the African economy as rising/growing, specifying this third reason of ASF's emergence entails asking the question of "what facilitates ASF optimism/utopianism?". I will focus on this question in the next section.

4. *D to U*, Afro-optimism, and the global financial crisis

Some years after the global financial crisis of 2007-8, the *Economist* (*Econ*) started producing an Afro-optimist discourse in a series of articles with titles such as "The Hopeful Continent: Africa Rising" (2011), "Africa's Hopeful Economies: the Sun Shines Bright" (2011), and "A Hopeful Continent" (2013). Econ was neither the first nor the only one to do so, but was arguably the most influential, popularising, if not introducing, the term "hopeful continent" in this context. According to *Econ*, there is no longer cause for the Afro-pessimist discourse to which it had long contributed, because "*this time the continent really is on the rise*" (cited in Havnevik, 2015:3). Three factors are contributing to this rise: The number of violent conflicts is declining, there is demographic and, more importantly, economic growth. *Econ* continues that Africa is the "world's fastest-growing continent […] not least thanks to foreign investments" (*Econ* 2011:6). It justifies its Afro-optimism saying that, unlike in the Americas and Europe,

Africa showed "great *resilience*" (cited in Havnevik, 2015:3) during the GFC.

A 2009 report from the African Development Bank (ADB) confirms that Africa was "shielded from the [...] negative effects of a financial crisis" in 2007 and 2008. However, it also adds that this was mainly because "financial markets are still underdeveloped and even non-existent in many [African] countries" (2009:ii). The ADB and, later, in an extensive report, Alabi et al., add that there is not much reason for optimism; the effects of the GFC on Africa were "largely underestimated" and had caused a decline in export, in inflow of foreign aid, and had cut economic growth in half (Alabi, 2011:16). While demonstrating some awareness thereof, *Econ* considers it no grounds for pessimism, bearing in mind the recessions elsewhere.

Kjell Havnevik, asking whether the *Econ*'s form of Afro-optimism is "realistic", addresses the friction between the accounts of *Econ* and ADB/Alabi et al. (2015:1). He shows that violent conflicts have been solved but that new ones have started, that there is demographic growth but that no labour market is created to sustain it, and that there is economic growth, but that thinking it will "trickle down and take care of poverty reduction" is "a repetition of the faulty logic of the 1960s" (13). Economic growth, he says, generally does not lead to "substantial reduction of poverty levels" (6) but benefits small groups of nationals and foreign investors, who profit from the favourable taxation in part imposed by organisations such as the OECD, the IMF, the World Bank, and so on. Hence, it is unrealistic to sustain the "narrative of Afro-optimism [...] beyond the next decade, since the current growth does not seem to lead to structural change, which can widen the productive base of African economies and benefit the majority of the continent's people" (7). Instead, Havnevik says, *Econ*'s Afro-optimism must be understood as a "narrative [...] to convince foreign investors that Africa had matured to become a 'safe terrain' for investments in natural resources, energy and land" (15) thus "legitimising the continued exploitation of Africa" (19).

For Havnevik, *Econ*'s Afro-optimism is unrealistic from the perspective of the African population—although it may be from the perspective of investors. Nonetheless, the previous section suggests that this form of Afro-optimism, complexly, does play into ASF. This is evident from the plots in which the poor overthrow the (mostly) rich in power—possibly related, ultimately, to an understanding of Africa's economy as growing, or the possibility thereof, at the expense of currently rich nation-states/organisations. It is evident also from the ASF discourse, in which the African economy is perceived as growing to the extent that the continent is likened to an awakening giant and to the emerging British Empire. Finally, one could wonder if Wood's use of the term "Hopeful Continent", a phrase he appears to quote in agreement, is accidental.

I want to emphasise that this does not mean, necessarily, that *Econ*'s and ASF's Afro-optimism are the same, if only because the former advocates the exploitation of the continent and the latter imagines the end of (primarily economic) domination. What I am suggesting is that it is not unlikely that *Econ*'s form of Afro-optimism contributed to a discursive environment in which a utopian ASF form could emerge. Especially considering that *Econ*'s Afro-optimism has spread widely, in the process has been (partly) disconnected from its original producers/context of production, and was rendered ideologically neutral to some degree (already visible in *Econ*'s articles on the topic), it is not unlikely that its content as analysed by Havnevik is not evident to all those who adopt and reproduce it. I also want to emphasise that, even if ASF emerges in a discursive space which is partly created by *Econ*, there is no reason to assume that the narrative work ASF and *Econ* Afro-Optimism perform is not antonymic—that their juxtaposition does not constitute a *discursive struggle*.

I say that *Econ*'s form of Afro-optimism contributed to a discursive environment, because *Econ*'s Afro-optimism is itself the result of another event—the GFC. Nick Srnicek has argued that the GFC can be thought of not simply as another economic crisis, but as neoliberalism's "death blow" (2012:6). I prefer to think of this as neoliberalism's *fall/rise*, because death was followed almost immediately by resurrection. This *fall/rise* necessitated the need for an alternative economic logic. And while those alternatives, such as a *new* (maybe "green") *new* deal, were short-lived in actuality, they did interrupt, however briefly, the TINA-discourse, which had suppressed imagining other possible social systems to a degree, and had promoted the narrative dystopia. Thus, the *fall/rise* can also be understood as contributing to a discursive environment in which a utopian ASF form could emerge.

If ASF's emergence can be said to have occurred in part in the discursive space created by the GFC, this also informs the year of emergence—2007, the year in which the GFC started. It may also provide a perspective from which to historicise existing ASF analyses: Bould argues, for example, that the "aliens" in Okorafor's *Lagoon* (2014) and Tade Thompson's *Rosewater* (2016) "represent the opportunity for a radical break

— and with it an alternative future free from the shackles of neoliberal developmentalism and carbon-imperialism" (Bould 2017:8). In the next section, the last before the conclusion, I will substantiate this ASF-GFC connection by showing in more detail what I consider the main characteristics of the *D to U*, and by addressing some of the above-mentioned ASF examples in more detail.

5. The seemingly dystopian narrative utopia (*D to U*)

The principal narrative and plot devices of the *D to U* form are: A social break or change, often a departure from a (allegorical capitalist) dystopian society that is claimed to be eternal, to a society that is considered better, and which may be located outside of narrative time. Narratively, this may take shape as changing narrators, locations, times, and so on. The change often entails a revolt against a dominant system or (often wealthy) ruling group (as opposed to individuals). The success of the revolt is at first claimed to be unlikely, a claim that is subsequently refuted, making characters (and readers) believe in the revolution's imminent success/chance of succeeding. Underprivileged social groups (as opposed to individuals), frequently the poor, are often the driving force behind these revolutions. Narratively, the focus on a group may take shape through forms of multi-strand narration, which decentres individual protagonists. Individuals may also revolt alone, and may be sacrificed/sacrifice themselves in the process. The *D to U* as such distinguishes itself from the narrative anti-utopian tradition, which is predominantly preoccupied with exploring the dangers of alternative social structures (e.g. totalitarian regimes), with reconstructing/upholding the destroyed society and/or its values (e.g. individualism, freedom), or with constructing a "good" capitalism, and which predominantly has single protagonists (a hero) and single enemies (evil person/corporation). Such dystopian narratives may serve as explicitly referenced counterpoints in *D to U* narratives. *D to U* narratives may contain all or some of these characteristics, as I will proceed to show in the examples below.

In the film *Pumzi*, botanist protagonist Asha lives in a seemingly dystopian, totalitarian, underground society after WWIII destroys the outside world. Dreaming is prohibited. But, when Asha analyses a plant seed called "our truth", she falls asleep and dreams about the possibility of a different world. A surveillance system wakes her and commands her to take her dream suppressors, but she requests the authorities for permission to search for the dream world instead. They tell her, in a variation on the neoliberal slogan of *there is no alternative*, that "the outside is dead". Disbelieving that claim, Asha goes out, finds that the place she dreamed about is real and, sacrificing herself, grows a tree successfully, thus creating the possibility of a new society and eliminating the necessity of her current dystopian one.

In Olukotun's *Nigerians in Space* (2014), the *D to U* movement is directly reminiscent of *Econ*'s Afro-optimism. Its chapters are divided into those that take place in 1993 and those in the "present day". In the former, a Nigerian space program fails. In the latter, the protagonist of the former sacrifices himself so his son can invent a sustainable and affordable light source (266). This foreshadows the space travel that will eventually take place in part two (and presumably three) of the *NiS* trilogy, and symbolically breaks with the 1993 part, in which the "possibilities" to "leapfrog the global

North" could not yet materialise (281).

In Towfik's *Utopia*, "two societies have formed: one of them owns everything and the other owns nothing" (2009:82), a result from the rich making "their money from the Others' [the poor] flesh, – from their dreams, their hopes, their pride and their health" (12). *Utopia*, then, echoes the production of inequality under capitalism, in which wealth in one place grows at the expense of poverty in another, a process that has arguably intensified under neoliberalism compared to Keynesianism. It is suggested that this situation cannot change: "Revolutions today", one character says, are ineffective. They are "more like riots, then helicopters hover in the air, launch some grenades and fire several shots, and the crowds disperse" (94). One character, Abd el-Zahir, continuously discusses a plan for a revolution, which his peers consider an "insane obsession [...], intellectual masturbation [...], he wouldn't do anything at all" (50). However, when the (poor) protagonist is murdered, the Others jointly execute El-Zahir's plan, isolate the rich from their resources, and storm their gated community.

Sansal's *2084. The End of the World* (2015) responds to the narrative dystopia explicitly. As the title implies, the novel follows George Orwell's *1984* (1948), whose protagonist cannot escape his dystopian society. *2084* describes the dystopian society of Abistan, which was built on the ruins of "Angsoc, or Angsok" (i.e. *1984*'s society) after Abistan had "drowned [Angsok in its] own blood" in a nuclear battle (221). Abistan's existence is reproduced by a discourse claiming there is no alternative society possible: "Abistan is Abistan and will remain Abistan" (234). However, in stark contrast to *1984*, *2084*'s protagonist is allowed to escape. This escape is captured in the ambiguity of the novel's title, which the dystopia-conditioned reader may easily understand as referring to the destruction of a society as it is known—as it would in, for instance, post-apocalyptic SF. However, the title instead refers to Abistan's claims of having no borders—of *being* the world, another variation of the TINA claim—and to the protagonist discovering that Abistan does end. The novel closes with him finding that Abistan is ruled by a rich elite, and with him crossing the end of the world and entering another, unknown one.

Efe Okogu's "Proposition 23" also explicitly departs from the narrative dystopia, and is perhaps best read as a rewriting of *Do Androids Dream of Electric Sheep* (Dick, 1968) or a preamble to *The Matrix* (1999), both of which it references (2012:382-400). The society of "23" is divided into "undead"/"undesirables" and "citizens" (371). Omelsky (2014) has pointed to the connection between "23"'s undead and the colonised subject. However, the society of "23" does not concern a colonial society (everyone can become undesirable), and the undead may equally well be understood through the concept of class, especially considering their poverty. This idea is supported by a character explaining that, "for every citizen who has minimum credit three others must become undead" (2012:388), explaining the social division along the lines of capitalism's logic as in *Utopia* above. Similar to *Utopia*, too, is the "rise" of the "undead" at the end of the narrative (376). In the multi-strand narration of "23", the undead rise as a class (unlike in the messianic *The Matrix*), destroy the undead/citizen division, and open up the possibility for an alternate society (unlike *Sheep*, which keeps the status quo intact).

It appears that, a decade after the emergence started, *D to U* maintains it prominence, and one could consider whether this is facilitated by a discourse characterising ASF writing as possibly subversive. ASF author Okorafor even claims, "science fiction is one of the greatest and most effective forms of political writing" (2017:1). Nevertheless, it is likely that as the body of ASF works grows, ASF's aesthetic forms and functions diversify. This may entail different narrative structures and themes altogether, and may already be noticed in the prominence of the topos of cyber-enhancement. But diversification also entails novel *D to U* forms, an example of which can be found in Joan de la Haye's "The Trial", which narrates a society in which "useless" people are killed by government decree to save sparse water. Protagonist Marin Brown, a writer of fiction and "very good breeding stock" (2012:272), is sentenced to death because there is no "room in [her] society for yet another mediocre author" (274). Briefly hoping that "the judge would change his mind", she knows "those hopes were futile" (274), and the story ends with Marin's beheading. The narrative is clearly a dystopian extrapolation of contemporary concerns about overpopulation, climate, and resources, but its main narrative work lies in breaking with the happy-ending tradition. The narrator-protagonist of "The Trial" offers very little possibility to be emotional about her death, as her narration lacks affective elements to trigger such a response. There are no sad thoughts; instead, there is relief and curiosity about what is to come. "The Trial", then, breaks with the anti-utopian tradition by disconnecting it from a narrative element and, not unlike the narratives above, replacing it with an afterlife yet unknown.

6. Conclusion

In summary, I suggest that several elements contributed to creating the space for ASF to emerge. These include the genre's increased distance to colonialism, and the increased access to mobile technology on the African continent that could facilitate the independent and "off-the-grid" circulation and consumption of ASF, and could show its market value to established publishers. It also includes the perceived democratisation of technology, and the GFC, or the *fall/rise* of neoliberalism. That event caused the perceived unequal distribution of the GFC's negative effects and the momentary interruption of the TINA discourse and associated genres such as the dystopian one. In turn, this could allow for different forms of Afro-optimism to emerge, as well as for the possibility of a novel utopian genre, which I preliminarily characterised as *D to U*. Hence, I consider ASF *inter alia* a reaction to the dystopian genre, and a separate phase in the joint history of SF/Utopia.

Given the broadness of the scope of this essay, none of the issues addressed here are presented in their full complexity, and all of them would benefit from further elaboration: Many questions remain about independent (digital) publishing, ASF'S techno-optimism, and the relation between colonialism and colonial ESF/AmSF, on the one hand, and ASF on the other. Most importantly, a more thorough analysis of ASF and its relation to Afro-Optimism is necessary, not least to unpack its ideological position and background, and the way that it is implicated in the world-system in which it is produced—particularly in light of some of the claims made about ASF's transformative potential. Finally, due to my scope, I have not addressed many of the individual, national, and regional reasons that may play into ASF's emergence. For example, some authors have pointed to the "whiteness" of the SF genre, and their desire to read African SF as a reason for writing ASF. Towik's *Utopia* is related to the social anxieties preceding the 2011 Egyptian *January 25 Revolution*, and it is possible that the events sometimes referred to as the *Arab Spring* may also be of importance to ASF. I will address these issues at a later time. For now, it must suffice to say that ASF appears to be changing African literature.

Work Cited

African Development Bank, 2009. *Impact of the Global Financial and Economic Crisis on Africa*. Econ Office of the Chief Economist.

Alabi et al., 2011. *Africa and the Global Financial Crisis: Impact on Economic Reform Processes*. Münster: Lit Verlag.

Aldiss, B., 1973. *Billion Year Spree: The True History of Science Fiction*. Garden City, N.Y.: Doubleday.

Anderson, P., 2004. *The River of Time*. New Left Review. 26. pp. 66–77.

Arigbabu, A., 2013. *Lagos_2060*. Lagos: Dada books.

Ashiru, AM., 2013. "Amphibian Attack". In: A. Arigbabu *Lagos_2060*. Lagos: Dada books. pp. 2–41.

Beaulieu, MC., 2016. *The Sea in the Greek Imagination*. Philadelphia: U of Pennsylvania P.

Bould, M., 2017. African Science Fiction. *Los Angeles Review of Books*, [e-magazine] 2 October. Available at: <https://lareviewofbooks.org> [Accessed 12 November 2017].

Clute, J. and Nicholls, P., 1993. *The Encyclopedia of Science Fiction*. London: Orbit.

Cohen, M. 1999. *The Sentimental Education of the Novel*, Princeton (NJ): Princeton University Press.

Csicsery-Ronay Jr., I., 2003. "Marxist Theory and Science Fiction." *The Cambridge Companion to Science Fiction*. U of Cambridge Press.

Dila, D., 2015. Is Science Fiction Really Alien to Africa? DilmanDila, [blog] 22 July. Available at: <http://www.dilmandila.com/2015/07/science-fiction-literature-africa-sff.html> [Accessed 3 September 2017].

Delany, S., 2011. *Silent Interviews on Language, Race, Sex, Science Fiction, and some Comics*. Hanover, London: U of New England P.

Dorman, N., 2015. *Terra Incognita*. South Africa: Short Story Day Africa.

Havnevik, K., 2015. The Current Afro-optimism – A Realistic Image of Africa? *Fleks*, 2(2), Pp. 1–19.

Haye, J., 2012. The Trial. In: I.W. Hartmann. *AfroSF*. StoryTime. pp. 268–276.

Kiregyera, B., 2015. *The Emerging Data Revolution in Africa*. Stellenbosch: SunPress.

Koschorke, Klaus, et al., 2007. *A History of Christianity in Asia, Africa, and Latin America, 1450-1990: A Documentary Sourcebook*. Wm. B. Eerdmans Publishing.

Levitas, R., 2007. Looking for the Blue: The Necessity of Utopia. *Journal of Political Ideologies*, 12(3). pp. 289–306.

Luckhurst, R. 2005. *Science Fiction*. Cambridge: Polity Press.

Moretti, F., 2000. Conjectures on World Literature. *New Left Review*, 1. pp. 54–68

Okogu, E., 2012. Proposition 23. In: I.W. Hartmann. *AfroSF*. StoryTime. pp. 352–405.

Okorafor, N., 2014. African Science Fiction is still Alien. *Wahala Zone*, [blog] 15 January. Available at: <http://nnedi.blogspot.co.uk/2014/01/african-science-fiction-is-still-alien.html?q=Tchidi+Chikere> [Accessed 3 September 2017].
---, 2017. Sci-fi Stories that Imagine a Future Africa. *TedTalk*, August 2017. Available at: <https://www.ted.com/talks/nnedi_okorafor_sci_fi_stories_that_imagine_a_future_africa/transcript>.

Olukotun, DB., 2014. *Nigerians in Space*. Los Angeles: Unnamed Press.

Omelsky, M., 2014. "After the End Times": Postcrisis African Science Fiction. *Cambridge Journal of Postcolonial Literary Inquiry*, 1(1), pp. 33–49.

Onwualo, C., 2016. African Science Fiction and Literature. *Omenana*, [e-magazine] 7 August. Available at: <https://omenana.com/2016/08/07/essay-african-science-fiction-and-literature/> [Accessed 3 September 2017].

Pumzi, 2009. [film] Directed by Wanuri Kahiu. Kenya: Focus Features.

Rieder, J., 2012. *Colonialism and the Emergence of Science Fiction*. Middletown, Con.: U of Wesleyan P.

Roberts, A., 2006. *The History of Science Fiction*. Houndmills, Basingstoke, Hampshire/New York: Palgrave.

Ryman, G., 2017a. 21 Today: The Rise of African Speculative Fiction. *Manchester Review*, [e-journal] 18. Available through Manchester Review website <http://www.themanchesterreview.co.uk/?p=8001> [Accessed 3 August 2017].

Sansal, B., 2015. *2084. The End of the World*. New York: Europa Editions.

Sargent, LT., 1976. Themes in Utopian Fiction in English Before Wells. *Science Fiction Studies*. 3(3). pp. 275–282.

Srnicek, N., 2012. Navigating Neoliberalism: Political Aesthetics in an Age of Crisis. *The Matter of Contradiction: Ungrounding the Object*, [presentation] 8–9 September. Available at: <www.wdw.nl/files/Navigating_Neoliberalism_Political_Aesth.pdf>

The Economist., 2011. Africa's hopeful economies: The Sun Shines Bright. *The Economist*, 3 Dec. pp. 82–84.

Towfik, AK., 2011 [2009]. *Utopia*. Doha: Bloomsbury Qatar Foundation Publishing.

Wood, N., 2009. SF in South Africa. *The World SF Blog*, [blog] 7 December. Available at: <https://worldsf.wordpress.com/2009/12/07/monday-original-content-sf-in-south-africa-by-nick-wood/> [Accessed 3 September 2017].
---2012. Africa in Science Fiction. *The World SF Blog*, [blog] 3 December. Available at: <https://worldsf.wordpress.com/2012/12/03/monday-original-content-africa-in-science-fiction-by-nick-wood/> [Accessed 3 September 2017].

---, 2016, *Azanian Bridges, Alconbury Weston:* Newcon Press

Zvomuya, P., 2015. Science Fiction and Blackness. *OkayAfrica*, [e-magazine] 28 October. Available at: <http://www.okayafrica.com/science-fiction-and-blackness-raimi-gbadamosi-on-african-futures/> [Accessed 3 September 2017].

Forces Shaping the Development of South African speculative fiction down the ages

By Nick Wood

I outline an overview of the production of written South African (SA) science or speculative fiction (SF) through the ages, up until 2017. A socio-historical lens is adopted, as it is not possible to fully understand the development of SF within South Africa without appreciating the changing socio-political contexts, which continues to both shape and constrain the emergence of local SF. Finally, an attempt will be made to grapple with the thorny question of why black writers are still under-represented within the SF genre in South Africa. (For a fuller online account of the development of SF within the broader African continent, consider Bould, 2015).

1.1 So, where did it all begin?

Fully two years before the first appearance of Amazing Stories and Hugo Gernsback's coining of the notion of 'scientifiction,' a South African writer called Ferdinand Berthoud appeared in *Weird Tales*, 3(1) in January 1924, with a story called "The Man Who Banished Himself". Berthoud was to have a number of stories in the pulps over the years, including one perhaps more provocatively entitled – certainly from a contemporary perspective - "A white man never steals: A novelette of the South African veldt." This latter tale is a fascinating, if slightly disturbing read: the story's plot and characters, both black and white, twist and turn, in order to keep the veracity of the title intact - perhaps with some underlying authorial irony, perhaps not.

The first truly speculative story of Berthoud's was 'Webbed Hands', however, which appeared as a cover story in the *Strange Tales* issue of November 1931. This is part horror-story, but with an underlying pseudo-scientific premise that the 'brown savage' monster at the heart of the story who is committing murders in locations throughout Cape Town is the product of a 'renegade English promoter' and an unknown – perhaps 'unnatural' - mother from 'the centre of Africa' (171).

The central potential theme for this (white) South African speculative fiction appears to be a fear of both 'racial miscegenation' and possibly what lurks within 'central Africa' too. (To be fair to subtleties within Berthoud's story, as well as the socio-historical context of his writing, perhaps the 'real' monster is the white manipulator who gets his 'just desserts' in the end.) This theme was not an isolated one, within 'white' culture in South Africa, at the time.

A year after the publication of 'Webbed Hands', the psychologist R.W. Wilcocks, investigating the 'poor white problem' in South Africa under the Carnegie Commission, called for 'legislation which inflicts severe penalties on sexual intercourse between races.' (1932). One of Wilcocks' psychologist protégés, H.F. Verwoerd, obliged by becoming an architect in the National Party's introduction of *apartheid* in 1948, thus introducing a raft of racist legislation, including the aptly named 'Immorality Act', which was aimed at ensuring 'white racial purity' (and dominance).

1.2 South African SF During the Years of Apartheid

Science fiction in South Africa during the apartheid years was a relatively subdued arena, given the socio-political exigencies of the time. 'Black' writing was discouraged as a potential outlet for grievances and political action, with apartheid policies dividing educational resources to try and maintain a large skill divide between a deliberately less literate black 'underclass' and a more skilled white hegemony. Realist fiction was thus seen as more 'relevant' to exploring the issues of living in South Africa, with many (black) writers challenging the status quo having their works banned or censored, such as Can Themba and Lewis Nkosi – see Peter McDonald's (2009) 'The Literature Police' for more details.

However, a white English speaking South African writer, who published internationally during the sixties and seventies, was Claude Nunes, who wrote *Inherit the Earth* (1966); *Recoil* (1971) with his wife Rhoda and *The Sky Trapeze* (1980), with thematic foci covering concerns such as telepathic androids, aliens and 'how to live in peace' (Clute & Nicholls, 2017). Although it was good to see a South African writer breaking into the SF Western mainstream, these books were also noticeable for their apparent distance from local sociopolitical events.

One Afrikaans writer also bucking the trend against writing science fiction was Jan Rabie, who wrote a number of overtly science-fiction books, such as *Swart Ster oor die Karoo* (*Black Star over the Karoo*, 1957), *Die Groen Planeet* (*The Green Planet*, 1961) and *Die Hemelblom* (*The Heaven Flower*, 1971). Although these books also tended to mirror dominant Euro-American SF themes - such as space-travel and alien plants - Rabie, however, was also part of a movement of Afrikaner writers beginning to challenge the dominant discourse of apartheid, known as 'Die Sestigers' (The Sixty-ers), which included Andre Brink and Breyten Breytenbach.

As the political 'heat' within the country rose after the Soweto uprising and the death in detention of Steve Biko in the mid to late seventies, several books emerged of perhaps a more surreal/fantastic bent. Nobel Laureate John M. Coetzee's (1980) *Waiting for the Barbarians* is one such book, with a magistrate caught between the brutal forces of Empire and the 'barbarians' supposedly waiting to invade. The censors suspected the book of being a thinly veiled allegorical allusion to both the apartheid state (as 'Empire') and the gathering forces of revolution or 'swart gevaar' (black danger), as the 'barbarians'. Coetzee's book, unlike Andre Brink's earlier *Kennis van die Aand* (*Looking on Darkness*, 1973), escaped a banning order.

Coetzee followed this up with a near-futuristic dystopia called *The Life and Times of Michael K* (1983), whereby a 'simple' hare-lipped gardener journeys to his mother's rural birth-place through civil-war torn South Africa.

Michael Cope's book *Spiral of Fire* (1987) is set during The State of Emergency in South Africa and uses a meta-fictional science fiction plot in order to juxtapose exploration of a First Contact peaceful 'alien culture', with the reality of military devastation unleashed upon burning black townships.

1.3 After Apartheid – What Next?

Following the demise of apartheid in the nineties, there was a freeing up of literary constraints, although always operating within the parameters of publishing and marketing decisions. 'Science fiction' has tended to be low in the priorities of local publishing houses and I have heard an editor state it does not have a significant black readership. This may to some extent be true – the legacy of apartheid means that education and even just generic reading and writing has had a huge equality backlog to catch up on between the 'white' and 'black' populations.

Furthermore, Science Fiction operates within a Western scientific discourse with tainted colonial associations and may perhaps be questioned both with regards to its relevance and its assumptions as to what is 'real' or central to lived experience in Africa. (Various religious and traditional/supernatural/alternative epistemological beliefs are still dominant *across the world*, as well as Africa. For an excellent discussion on relevance, see Nnedi Okorafor's online post – 'Is Africa ready for science fiction?' (2009).

Notwithstanding this, I think there are promising swells in a growing South African wave of science - or perhaps speculative fiction - in its broadest sense. The importance of introducing a new and younger generation to this genre cannot be over emphasised. Thus the increasing tide of the popularity of Young Adult fiction in the West, perhaps being somewhat replicated in Africa, is of significance.

2.1 Young Adult SF in South Africa

For Young Adult (YA) readers for example, there have been 'South African flavoured' SF books such as: Peter Wilhelm's *Summer's End* (1984); Elana Bregin's *The Slayer of Shadows* (1995); Peter Slingsby's *The Joining* (1996); Robin Saunders' *Sons of Anubis* (1998); Jenny Robson's *Savannah 2216 AD* (2004); Nick Wood's *The Stone Chameleon* (2004); Lesley Beake's *Remembering Green* (2009); Adeline Radloff's *Sidekick* (2010); Lily Herne's 'Deadlands' Trilogy (2010); Charlie

Human's *Apocalypse Now Now* (2013) and Helen Brain's 'Elevation' trilogy (2016 – to date) amongst others. On the other side of the Limpopo River, although she is now US resident, there was Nancy Farmer's Zimbabwean based *The Ear, The Eye and The Arm* (1995). Of note, however, is that very few of these books involve black writers, or a targeted black readership.

Apostolides (2016) has pointed out the importance of Young Adult fantasies and speculative fiction literature, which not only fuels the imagination of the younger generation in South Africa, but helps to develop multi-cultural awareness and alternative ways of seeing things. Getting these books into schools is thus of paramount concern, as this will help to foster literacy that validates the use of speculative fiction as a genre worth time and respect.

2.2 Adult SF in South Africa

1. Short Fiction

With regards to adult writing, there has been a South African 'science fiction and horror' magazine called *Something Wicked*, which has published short fiction by writers such as Sarah Lotz, Dave de Beer, Abi Godsell and Richard Kunzmann in its initial ten issues, with several more online/digital issues appearing subsequently. (Richard Kunzmann, although he is Namibian born, has also written a trilogy of excellent South African crime thrillers with speculative-fiction elements, starting with *Bloody Harvests*)

Something Wicked (SW), which proved to be instrumental in launching the careers of more than a few genre writers, eventually moved from a monthly edition to an annual anthology. Unfortunately, SW appears to be on hiatus currently, and nothing has emerged since the Volume 2 anthology in 2013.

Another South African magazine still 'alive' and worth pursuing is *Jungle Jim*, with 26 issues of Pan-African fiction to date, including SF short stories from the likes of Suyi Davies (Nigeria), Jonathan Dotse (Ghana), Chinelo Onwualu (Nigeria), Liam Kruger (South Africa), and Masimba Masodza (Zimbabwe).

Operating for a mammoth 171 issues and counting, however, is the Science Fiction and Fantasy Society of South Africa's (SFSA) magazine *Probe*, which has been in existence since 1969. Probe publishes both winners and runners up from its annual science fiction short story competition called the '*Novas*' and has published stories by writers such as W.G. Lipsett, Gerhard Hope, Arthur Goldstuck, Liz Simmons, and Yvonne Walus, as well as three collections of short stories from *Probe*, entitled *The Best of South African Science Fiction*.

A worthy collection of perhaps specifically broader African speculative/science fiction was published within *Chimurenga* magazine's double issue (12&13), *Doctor Satan's Echo Chamber*. Further, with regards to African writing, a South African short story that won the 2008 Caine Prize for best African writing in English was called "Poison", written by Henrietta Rose-Innes; a story which was set just outside a post-apocalyptic Cape Town.

There have been other science fiction stories published internationally by South African SF writers: Lavie Tidhar, for instance, spent a considerable period of time in South Africa and his "Bophuthatswana", appearing in Farah Mendlesohn's

Glorifying Terrorism (2006), has clear South African concerns, delivered in localised language.

Probably the best current venue for South African short fiction, with a specifically SF bent, is Short Story Day South Africa (SSDA), with their annual competition anthologising high quality literature from across the African continent. Their specifically SF anthology, *Terra Incognita*, was reviewed warmly in the pages of the Los Angeles Review of Books by the critic Mark Bould (2015b).

2. Novels

One South African writer who has been productive for a couple of decades with both books and short fiction is Dave Freer, who has written solo – his first book, *The Forlorn*, was published in 1999 – as well as teaming up at various points with Eric Flint and Mercedes Lackey. Dave has also written a solid batch of novellas and short stories, some peculiarly and specifically South African; such as "Candyblossom", in T*he Best of Jim Baen's Universe* (2006). A South African based writer of Scottish origin, Paul Crilley, also publishes internationally, with a YA novel, *Rise of the Darklings* (2010), and an adult SF book, *Poison City* (set in Durban, 2016), amongst others.

Two other significant books that initially explored the South African landscape via SF sensibilities, as bifurcated by the urban-rural divide, are Jane Rosenthal's *Souvenir* (2004) and Lauren Beukes' debut, *Moxyland* (2008). The hip multimedia style of *Moxyland* includes an accompanying urban soundtrack – the book itself is written in a fast paced style, steeped in South African language and within a near-future dystopian Cape Town separated by corporate rather than racist apartheid. The term 'apartheid' itself is not used within the novel, as far as I am aware, which carries its history lightly but cleverly as it moves rapidly between shifting perspectives and ways of communicating towards its moving climax. *Zoo City*, Lauren's Johannesburg based follow-up, was even better, going on to win the Arthur C. Clarke Award in 2011.

Likewise, there is much to recommend Jane Rosenthal's *Souvenir* – a meditation on the diverse South African landscape and the mirrored shaping impact on relationships of the future. The narrative follows the work of a 'barbiclone' in the latter half of the twenty-first century as she balloons above the desert-like hinterland of the Karoo, down to the coast, where a giant tsunami awaits, driven by collapsing ice-shelves from Antarctica. Although significantly slower than *Moxyland*, the pace is sufficient for the story. (It's also good to see a major character of Nigerian heritage, who is also a sympathetically drawn character, in a South African product!)

In Afrikaans, Eben Venter has written *Horrelpoot* (2006), now in translation as *Trencherman*, confronting a dystopian South African future. Finally, and not least of all - although it's not strictly science fiction – South African 'magical realism' certainly fits under the speculative fiction umbrella. For me, the pre-eminent South African writer here is Zakes Mda, who has written a spate of works, of which *The Heart of Redness* and *The Whale Caller* are particularly inspiring. Although Mda writes mainly within a 'realist' frame, many of his novels contain fantastic/'magical' elements. Indeed, Mda has mentioned previously that Gabriel Garcia Marquez told him 'magical realism' in his own work had been influenced by the historical presence of African slaves, carrying this tradition within their own oral storytelling culture. The forces shaping literature have always been fluid and global.

Although written some years ago now, a favourite of mine from the Mda oeuvre remains *The Heart of Redness* (2000), set in the Eastern Cape, with parallel tales of modern and nineteenth century concerns focused around the mass starvation of the amaXhosa. This was amongst those who followed the prophetic calling of Nongqawuse, the prophetess who spread her vision that the dead would rise to expel the colonialists should the amaXhosa have faith and kill their own cattle. This book weaves together past and present, faith and myth, in a resonant tapestry that made me weep for home, while reading it on the far shores of Aotearoa New Zealand.

As Gerald Gaylard argues, 'the 'liberated imagination' in these stories of the fantastic may also provide the basis for resolving many complex issues within postcolonial Africa (2005). The creative imagination of these texts allows for alternative socio-political realities to be both envisaged and striven for. The development of South African SF gathered significant pace from 2011 onwards, with the work of Lauren Beukes in particular appearing to push open a door, if not yet floodgates. Also of note in 2011 was the start of the Arab Spring, and an increased mood of global optimism, that may have contributed towards the sense of growing change and creativity.

3. The Partial Flowering of South African SF, from 2011 Onwards

2011 and immediately beyond were vigorous years for South African speculative fiction, as it gathered further pace and push from the heralding, punchy impact of Lauren Beukes's first two SF novels in particular. 2011 was split almost mid-year by the *Arthur C. Clarke Award* being presented to Lauren's *Zoo City*, which helped raised the profile of SF in South Africa.

Either side of this seminal event for South African speculative fiction lay various SF/F/H publishing successes for a growing number of local South African authors.

Nerine Dorman has been doing sterling work in the indie horror world. She has published *The Namaqualand Book of the Dead* (Lyrical Press) and is the editor of the annual *Bloody Parchment* anthology. She also collaborates with Carrie Clevenger on a humorous paranormal/vampiric romance series (the first one is called *Just my Blood Type*).

The *Pornokitsch.com* publishers – Anne Perry and Jared Shurin - launched *Pandemonium: Stories of the Apocalypse* (2011), with excellent stories in it from a host of SA writers (Sam Wilson, Lauren Beukes, Charlie Human and SL Grey). The Irish SF magazine *Albedo One* (Issue 40) published Nick Wood's alternative history story "Bridges", set in a contemporary South Africa where apartheid has survived. [This story was subsequently extended to become the novel *Azanian Bridges* (2016).]

Diane Awerbuck's highly-lauded short story collection, *Cabin Fever*, includes a wonderfully creepy and psychologically disturbing story featuring the *Mami Wata*. When Diane tackles spec fiction, she does it superbly. Additionally, although not strictly horror/spec, Louis Greenberg wrote of Henrietta Rose-Innes's *Nineveh*:

> *Henrietta Rose-Innes, the Caine Prize-winning author of 'Poison', a story about a post-apocalyptic Cape Town, released her third novel, Nineveh, this year. Nineveh is what you might*

> *call subtle-spec, an ostensibly literary novel that gets weird when a plague of bugs takes over a hubristic new housing development south of Cape Town. In all her work, Rose-Innes is preoccupied with archaeology: digging away layers of history and meaning, and set squarely in contemporary South Africa and Cape Town where reality is often too bizarre and frightening to fictionalise, it is inevitable that strange things emerge from her imaginative excavations.* (cited in Lotz, Wood, Barben, 2011).

Newer work from Rose-Innes includes *Green Lion* (2015), a haunting work of eco-fiction set in Cape Town.

Furthermore, Andrew Salomon was short-listed for the *Terry Pratchett Prize* for his novel *Lun*, which explored a variety of themes, including the smart and funny notion of a 'sanctuary for tokoloshes'. Tom Learmont's *Light across Time* (Kwela Books) explored a novel evolutionary idea for extra-terrestrials, back-dropped amongst a heady mix of zany theories and meticulously researched historical events.

Ken Sibanda's *The Return to Gibraltar* was a welcome and enterprising SF debut by a black South African author – although he is also a naturalised American now (Proteus Books). The novel involves an African American protagonist time-traveling to 1491 to help the Spanish Moors resist the Christian 'reconquista'. SL Grey's *The Mall* (Corvus UK) was a dark and at times savage exploration of the life underneath (or parallel to, or even within) shopping malls, as experienced by a young white man and black woman, thrown unwillingly together by who knows what – or whom…

Also making an appearance in February 2012 was Cat Hellisen's internationally published *When the Sea is Rising Red* (WTSIRR), followed by *The House of Sand and Secrets* (2013).

Although categorised as YA fiction, WTSIRR is undoubtedly a crossover novel, and its political undertones and cliché-smashing heroine have already been much praised by reviewers. Cat's *Beastkeeper* (2015) was another wonderful YA fantasy follow-up and her beautiful short stories – published in the likes of *Shimmer* and *Fantasy and Science Fiction* – are to be collated in an anthology entitled '*Learning How to Drown*' – due to be published by NewCon Press in 2018.

And, against this growing and exciting brew of South African SF writers, Lauren Beukes secured a spectacular hat-trick of book deals for her next novel, *The Shining Girls* (2013), and continues to push the SF envelope with her subsequent sequence of comics, novels, and short stories (*Slipping*, 2016).

The end of 2012 also saw the launch of Ivor Hartmann's *AfroSF* – the first ever African anthology of SF, with SA writers such as Mandisi Nkomo, Christy Zinn, Mia Arderne, Sarah Lotz, Liam Kruger, Sally Partridge, and Nick Wood represented. This ground-breaking anthology has been critically appraised by Omelsky (2014), Yaszek (2014), and Moonsamy (2016).

While stalwart local publishers such as Umuzi, Jacana, and Kwela were beginning to open their doors to more speculative fare, local digital publishers also moved into the SF scene – namely Fox & Raven, who have published work by Martin Stokes, Mia Arderne, and Dave de Burgh, amongst others – as well as 'wordsmack', who have published Abi Godsell's *Idea War*. The excitement generated by Lauren Beukes's Clarke Award success added to a growing confluence of South African SF, in both print and online format (Bridle, 2015).

Jacana published Thando Mgqolozana's second book, *Hear Me Alone* (2011), described as 'an African makeover of

Judea'. Moving more clearly within genre boundaries, Charlie Human's *Apocalypse Now Now* (2013) is a zany, humorous melange of fantasy and local myth, within the supernatural underworld of Cape Town, followed up by *Kill Baxter* (2014). Alex Latimer's *The Space Race* (2013) follows the tale of an old apartheid era South African nuclear capability, and the first African spaceship to launch beyond the Earth. Other local writers include Rachel Zadok (*Sister Sister*, 2013) and Sam Wilson, whose *Zodiac* (2016) is currently causing waves.

The collaboration behind the horror writing of SL Grey has long been known. Sarah Lotz's partner in horrific crime is Louis Greenberg, who is both an editor and a beautiful writer – see his 'Mummy' story, "Akhenaten Goes to Paris", in *The Book of the Dead* – and his edgy alternative South Africa in *Dark Windows* (2015).

Sarah Lotz herself has joined Lauren Beukes at the forefront of South African SF – her novels *The Three* (2014), *Day Four* (2015), and *The White Road* (2017) are gathering large international interest, and attract attention from the likes of Stephen King.

Other recent SF books of significance are Fred Strydom's *The Raft* (2015), Andrew Miller's *Dub Steps* (2015), Nikhil Singh's *Taty Went West* (2016), Nick Wood's *Azanian Bridges* (2016), and Gavin Chait's *Lament for the Fallen* (2016), and *Our Memory Like Dust* (2017), all of which attest to a significant and diverse flowering of South African SF in the twenty-tens. But one question of significance remains: *Why is South African SF still so predominantly white?*

4. On Whiteness in South African Speculative Fiction

In May 2015, Thando Mgqolozana left the almost exclusively white publishing landscape within South Africa to try and help foster black publishing initiatives and ventures. Mgqolozana (2015) pointed out the ongoing colonial nature of publishing within South Africa and, with white ownership retained, the predominance of writers nurtured would almost inevitably be white. He made links with the *Rhodes Must Fall Movement* (2015), which called for the decolonisation of South Africa, including its literary establishment. Mgqolozana (2015b) went on to outline 21 propositions for decolonising South African publishing spaces, which involved developing a separate and black-centred publishing arena. The establishment of the *Abantu Book Festival* in Soweto has been one productive development of this enterprise.

It was no accident that when I first approached publishers in South Africa about my YA SF novel, *The Stone Chameleon* (2004), I was told '*black people don't read science fiction*' – a statement aimed at my book, given black characters and some township settings were used within. Given this publication bias, it is no wonder white writers have been predominantly fostered, and that specifically (black) African perspectives on SF have been relatively hard to engender. Furthermore, white privilege and capital continues to operate within South Africa, a problem exacerbated by the South African state itself also failing to deliver on the economic (and educational/literacy) transformation promised, following the optimistic and heady Mandela years of the late nineteen-nineties.

Muzenda (2017) notes that, '*We know that (black) Africans need to tell their own stories, but it is just as important that we are allowed to imagine our own futures.'*

A 2016 report by Fireside Fiction, from America, stated that only 1.96% percent of the science fiction stories in 2015 were written by black authors (Liptak, 2016). With the majority of these stories originating from the United States of America, it begs the question: how much representation do African writers have in that 1.96%? (Muzenda, 2017).

In a 2014 essay, "African science fiction is still alien", published on her personal blog, Nigerian-American author Nnedi Okorafor reflects on why it's important for Africa to be represented in science-fiction, concluding: '1. Africans are absent from the creative process of global imagining that advances technology through stories. 2. Africans are not yet capitalising on this literary tool which is practically made to redress political and social issues.'

This message has been further reinforced by Wanuri Kahiu – Kenyan producer of the ground-breaking SF film *Pumzi* – who has emphasised both the marginalisation of black stories, but also the ancient centrality of SF within the African imagination, and the need to take ownership of the future through the expression of these stories (Chutel, 2016). In a continent full of cultures, religions and rich folklore, Africa is the perfect breeding ground for speculative fiction stories – not just stories set in Africa, but stories 'written *by* Africans *for* Africans' (Muzenda, 2017).

There are more black writers venturing into African speculative fiction. South Africa's Khaya Maseko recently published a science-fiction novella set in kwaMashu in KwaZulu-Natal, entitled *Mashu oMusha* (*The African Geek Girl*, 2017). Unathi Magubeni was shortlisted for the Etisalat Prize for his SF novella *Nwelezelanga: The Star Child* (2016).

Okorafor is the first black author to win the World Fantasy Award for Best Novel. The creation of the African Speculative Fiction Society in 2016, in conjunction with its Nommo Awards, is a big step in cementing and centring African authors in speculative fiction. (The inaugural Nommo Awards recently took place, having been announced at the Ake Literary Festival in Nigeria: Tor, 2017). *Omenana* Magazine, based in Nigeria, has also been facilitating the publishing of (black) African SF. Locally, a new isiZulu publishing company, *Kwasukela*, has launched a call for isiZulu speculative short fiction (Reading List, The, 2017).

The presence of these spaces – websites, magazines, and publications – goes a long way in introducing readers to different writers, and getting aspiring (black) authors the visibility they need. One of these people is Masimba Musodza, a Zimbabwean author and playwright currently based in the UK. Books were a part of his life from an early age, and science-fiction television shows were a big part of his childhood. Musodza wrote the first SF book in chiShona, entitled *MunaHacha Maive Nei?*. Musodza recalls, "The publishing industry as it is has its own ideas about African literature. There's a belief that Africans shouldn't write about such things (speculative fiction)." (Ryman, 2017a).

This rigid view of what constitutes an African story has hampered the growth of speculative fiction – the desire to write and read is there, but if publishing houses fail to validate this genre, home-grown speculative fiction will continue to suffer. Dave De Burgh (2015) has long argued along these lines, that SFF is still 'stifled' in South Africa, even to white writers.

The importance of the SF genre, in its broadest and most

all-encompassing sense, cannot be underestimated. For, as Muzenda (2017) states:

> *There is power in imagination and creativity, in conjuring something new and exciting from reality. Speculative fiction in all its shapes and forms allows both writer and reader to transport themselves into an alternate world, a space they can completely immerse themselves, a space they can claim for themselves. In a modern world where issues of representation, ownership and space are constantly coming under question, it's integral for African literature to be present in genres it was previously absent from.*

Conclusion

Although this is not a comprehensive South African overview, brief mention should be made at least of emerging literature in neighbouring countries, such as Zimbabwe – e.g. broadly speculative-fiction writers Dambudzo Marechera (who died young), Yvonne Vera, Ivor Hartmann, George Makana Clark, and Tendai Huchu. On the Indian Ocean coastal side of Zimbabwe, the magical realist writings of Mia Couto continue to illuminate the experiences of both humans and animals within Mozambique (Jaggi, 2015).

Couto himself mentions, 'I am white and African. I like to unite contradictory worlds.' So, to the full flowering of South African speculative fiction, both black and white, in the years and decades ahead. And to our SF forging an African future of hope, strength and diversity.

Work Cited

African Geek Girl, The, 2017. *Mashu oMusha and Black African Science Fiction*. [online]. Available through: <http://afroscifigirl.tumblr.com/post/157324997833/mashu-omusha-and-black-african-science-fiction> [Accessed 29th November 2017].

Apostolides, A., 2016. South African fantasy: Identity and spirituality. *HTS Teologiese Studies/Theological Studies*, 72(1), pp. 1-5.

Berthoud, F., 1924. The Man Who Banished Himself. *Weird Tales*, 3(1). Chicago: Rural Publications.

Berthoud, F., 1931. Webbed Hands. *Strange Tales*, November. Clayton Publications.

Bould, M., 2015a. *African Science Fiction 101*, February. [online]. Available through: <https://markbould.com/2015/02/05/african-science-fiction-101/> [Accessed 28th March 2017].

Bould, M., 2015a. *African Science Fiction 101: Update 1*, June: [online]. Available through: <https://markbould.com/2015/06/24/african-science-fiction-101-update/> [Accessed 28th July 2017].

Bould, M., 2015a. *African Science Fiction 101: Update 2*, December. [online]. Available through: <https://markbould.com/2015/12/12/african-science-fiction-101-update-2/> [Accessed 28th December 2017].

Bould, M., 2015b. If Colonialism Was The Apocalypse, What Comes Next? *Los Angeles Review of Books*. [online]. Available through: <https://lareviewofbooks.org/article/if-colonialism-was-the-apocalypse-what-comes-next-dilman-dila/> [Accessed 28th November 2017].

Bould, M., 2017. African Science Fiction. October, *Los Angeles Review of Books*. [online]. Available at: <https://lareviewofbooks.org/article/african-science-fiction/> [Accessed 29th November 2017].

Bridle, J., 2015. Why Africa is the New Home of Science Fiction. *The Guardian*. [online]. Available through: <https://www.theguardian.com/books/2015/jul/13/africa-science-fiction-afrocyberpunk-wordsmack-lauren-beukes> [(Accessed 29th November 2017].

Byrne, D., 2004. Science Fiction in South Africa. *PMLA*, 119 (3), pp. 522-525.

Chutel, L., 2016. Science fiction has ancient roots in Africa. Why shouldn't it also have a future there? *Quartz Africa*. [online]. Available through: <https://qz.com/743683/without-allowing-space-for-imagination-we-lose-hope/> [Accessed 29th November 2017].

Clute, J. and Nicholls, P., 2017. Claude Nunes. SFE: *The Encyclopedia of Science Fiction*. [online]. Available through: <http://www.sf-encyclopedia.com/entry/nunes_claude> [Accessed 22nd November 2017].

De Burgh, D., 2015. Why is SFF Stifled in South Africa? *SA Books Live*. [online]. Available through: <http://davebrendon.bookslive.co.za/blog/2015/12/14/why-is-sff-stifled-in-south-africa/> [Accessed 29th November 2017].

Gaylard, G., 2005. *After Colonialism: African Postmodernism and Magical Realism*. Johannesburg: Wits University Press.

Jaggi, M., 2015 Interview with Mia Couto. *The Guardian*. [online]. Available through: <https://www.theguardian.com/books/2015/aug/15/mia-couto-interview-i-am-white-and-african-i-like-to-unite-contradictory-worlds> [Accessed 29th November 2017].

Liptak, A., 2016. Science fiction publishing has a major race problem, new report shows. *The Verge*. [online]. Available through: <https://www.theverge.com/2016/8/4/12374306/science-fiction-diversity-numbers-fireside-report> [Accessed 29th November 2017].

Lotz, S., Wood, N., Barben, T., 2011. 2011 – A Year South African Speculative Fiction Gathers Momentum. *The World SF Blog*. [online].

Available through: <https://worldsf.wordpress.com/2012/03/12/2011-south-african-sff-in-review/> [Accessed 29th November 2017].

McDonald, P., 2009. *The Literature Police*. Oxford: Oxford University Press.

Moonsamy, N., 2016. Life Is a Biological Risk: Contagion, Contamination, and Utopia in African Science Fiction. *Cambridge Journal of Postcolonial Literary Inquiry*, 3(3), pp. 329–343. doi:10.1017/pli.2016.16

Mgqolozana, T., 2015a. Look at Yourselves; It's Very Abnormal. *SA Books Live Blog*, 18th May. [online]. Available through: <http://bookslive.co.za/blog/2015/05/18/look-at-yourselves-its-very-abnormal-thando-mgqolozana-quits-south-africas-white-literary-system/> [Accessed 29th November, 2017].

Mgqolozana, T., 2015b. Twenty One Suggestions for the Decolonisation of the South African Literary Scene, *SA Books Live*. [online]. Available through: <http://bookslive.co.za/blog/2015/05/19/thando-mgqolozana-outlines-21-suggestions-for-the-decolonisation-of-the-south-african-literary-scene/> [Accessed 29th November 2017].

Muzenda, M., 2017. Why is Science Fiction so White? *Daily Maverick*. [online]. Available through: <https://www.dailymaverick.co.za/opinionista/2017-03-15-why-is-science-fiction-so-white/#.WhVUQkpl_IU> [Accessed 28th November 2017].

Okorafor, N., 2009. Is Africa Ready for Science Fiction? *Wahala Zone Blog*. [online]. Available through: <http://nnedi.blogspot.co.uk/2009/08/is-africa-ready-for-science-fiction.html> [Accessed 28th November 2017].

Okorafor, N., 2014. African Science Fiction is still Alien. *Wahala Zone Blog*. [online]. Available through: <http://nnedi.blogspot.co.uk/2014/01/african-science-fiction-is-still-alien.html?q=Tchidi+Chikere> [Accessed 28th November 2017].

Omelsky, M., 2014. "After the End Times": Post-crisis African Science Fiction. *The Cambridge Journal of Postcolonial Literary Inquiry*, 1, pp. 33-49 doi:10.1017/pli.2013.2

Reading List, The (2017) New isiZulu publishing company Kwasukela Books launches with call for submissions. [online]. Available through: <https://readinglist.click/sub/new-isizulu-publishing-company-kwasukela-books-launches-with-call-for-submissions/> [Accessed 29th November 2017].

Ryman, G., 2017a. 100 Writers of African SFF. *Strange Horizons*. [online]. Available through: <http://strangehorizons.com/100-african-writers-of-sff/> [Accessed 29th November 2017].

Ryman, G., 2017b. 21 Today: The Rise of African Speculative Fiction. *The Manchester Review*, 18. [online]. Available through: <http://www.themanchesterreview.co.uk/?cat=343> [(Accessed 29th November 2017].

TOR (2017) Announcing the 2017 Nommo Award Winners. *Tor.Com*, November. [online]. Available through: <https://www.tor.com/2017/11/16/announcing-the-2017-nommo-award-winners/> [(Accessed 29th November 2017].

Wilcocks, R.W., 1932. *Psychological report: The poor white. Volume 2 of The Poor White Problem in South Africa. Carnegie Commission of Investigation on the Poor White Question in South Africa*. Pro ecclesia-drukkery.

Wood, N., 2009. SF in South Africa. *The World SF Blog*, December. [online]. Available through: <https://worldsf.wordpress.com/2009/12/07/monday-original-content-sf-in-south-africa-by-nick-wood/> [Accessed 29th November 2017].

Wood, N., 2015. Academia and the Advance of African Science Fiction. *Omenana*, 2. [online]. Available at: <https://omenana.com/2015/03/05/academia-and-the-advance-of-african-science-fiction/> [Accessed 29th November 2017].

Yaszek, L., 2014. Rethinking Apocalypse in African SF. *Paradoxa: Africa SF*. 25, pp. 47-66.

The Dangers of Expectation in African Speculative Fiction

By Ezeiyoke Chukwunonso

It was the 1960's. Chinua Achebe published his ground-breaking novel, Things Fall Apart, and there was a buzz about African literature globally. Writers like Ngugi wa Thiong'o, Bessie Head, Flora Nwakpa followed suit. The critics turned to them with a question: now that African literature had emerged, what was the world's expectation of this tradition? Achebe and co. then laid down the foundations of the boundaries that this new novel tradition would cover. It was to teach people who Africans really were, especially the West, who had construed Africans as salvagers. It was to be used to fight colonialism and neo-colonialism. Subsequently, African writers wrote to fit into this model. But this expectation had its pitfalls. Majorly, it constrained African literature from developing and growing into different sophisticated styles, themes, and genres. Helen Andrews articulated it thus:

> *African novel-writing has scarcely progressed since he (Chinua Achebe) inaugurated it with the celebrated Things Fall Apart. In the decades since that title was published [...] the American novel has evolved through a multitude of vogues and phases while the Anglophone African novel has, for the most part, remained as it was when Achebe launched it: unremarkable in its prose, flat in its characterization, anti-Western in its politics, and preoccupied with the confrontation between tradition and modernity."* (Andrews, 2017).

Recently, there was a shift that occurred in African literature which led currently to the growth of genre fiction in Africa. But what led to this shift? This essay will trace the history of that rise, hinting at what had held African literature to ransom and from growing for quite a long time, and especially on the damage of the "expectation syndrome". It will theorise on the pitfalls that African genre fiction would tend to avoid if it is to avoid its growth being ground to a standstill.

Introduction

The current boom in speculative fiction in Africa presupposes some pertinent ontological questions: why is this rise happening now? Does it imply that, prior to this current time, Africans didn't write genre fiction? Or, if they did, why was it a downplayed mode of art in both the continent and by her members in diasporas before this period? And what were the factors that necessitated this current surge of interest? Chinelo Onwualu found these questions nauseating when she wrote,

> Nearly every article on African speculative fiction that I've read starts with an air of surprise and discovery ... Or, if it is written by an African writer of the genre, it has an air of justification, with the author defending their interest ... Frankly, I'm tired of these sorts of articles. (Onwualu, 2016).

But then she realised that these ontological questions couldn't be resolved by merely wishing them away. It was like a stink perpetually clinging to the genre. Onwualu ended up taking the justification approach she attributed to African Writers of the genre, of which she is of course one, by citing Mark Bould's article "African Science Fiction 101" (2017), which historically traced speculative fiction in Africa even before World War 2. Geoff Ryman published a similar article to Bould's, which he titled "21 Today: The Rise of Speculative Fiction, year by year" (2017). Based on the evidence of Bould's research, Onwualu affirmed that, "Africans have been producing speculative fiction—that is, science fiction, fantasy, magical realism, et al.—since the genre began and the fact that people are just discovering it is really no one's fault but their own" (2016).

This *Justification-approach-of-Africa-genre theory* could only account for the fact that Africans had been engaging in speculative fiction for some time. However, it had nothing to say on the reason why this mode of writing had recently begun to garner interest from both fans and writers in Africa and the diasporas.

In addressing the reasons that gave birth to this boom, Onwualu wrote:

> ...*there has been a resurgence of African speculative fiction—perhaps starting in 2008, when the South African art journal Chimurenga published one of the first round-ups of African speculative art, and accelerated when Nnedi Okorafor won the World Fantasy Award for her 2010 novel Who Fears Death ... Genre fiction in North America [...] has been undergoing an internal upheaval ... A social justice movement that challenges the idea that speculative fiction is or should be the exclusive enclave of white, Anglo-American males ... Calls for diversity [...] have pushed fans to seek their stories from a wider pool, and that has gotten them looking in "unusual" places.* (Onwualu, 2016).

There are three main points she drew out here on why Africa genre fiction is booming:

1. The influence of *Chimurenga Journal*: there is no reason to withhold praise for the publication but one could argue that, before the issue of the magazine featuring speculative African art, there had already been ambitious speculative works from African writers, as can easily be seen in the interrelated articles of Bould (2015) and Ryman (2017). There were

novels like the *Famished Road* by Ben Okri, which had won him The Booker Award, and *Wizard of the Crow* by Ngugi wa Thiong'o, winner of the Finnish award for best science fiction novel. Even earlier than that, *The Palm-Wine Drunkard and his Dead Palm-Wine Tapster in the Dead's Town* by Amos Tutuola (1952) had dizzied the world, so much so that the Welsh poet Dylan Thomas gave it a rave review in *The Observer*. But none of these ignited the popularity of African SFF as it is currently being witnessed. What was it then that was so unique and special about Chimurenga's *roundups of African speculative art* that caused the radical change in the genre and made people take interest? Onwualu didn't answer this.

2. The second reason she gave was the effect of Nnedi Okorafor's World Fantasy Award. This was plausible because awards and recognition often draw attention to certain works. But then again, attention in most cases goes to the author rather than to the whole tradition that the writer writes from. Talking of African speculative fiction that had won prestigious awards which are even more renowned than Okorafor's, we come back to the *Famished Road* by Ben Okri. But this didn't draw attention to African Speculative fiction as a whole; it put the spotlight instead on Okri's writing. So, what was so different about Okorafor's award that it could stir this change?

3. The most problematic thing in Onwualu's article was the last point that she hinted at. She asserted that it was attention from the West, who were in conversation about the need for diversity in literature, that acted as the propelling force behind the rise of speculative fiction in Africa. In particular, let's focus on these words: "*Calls for diversity—in characters and writers—have pushed fans to seek their stories from a wider pool, and that has gotten them looking in "unusual" places.*" (2016). In other

words, when Western audiences craved diversity and sought this out in these "unusual" places, i.e. Africa, African writers jumped at the opportunity to become content providers for this appetite. In this lay the myth that African writers were performing for the West because there was no audience at home. This was not a new accusation for African literature. About 45 years ago, Chinua Achebe, talking about the same phenomenon, said:

> *I realise that a lot has been made of the allegation that African writers have to write for European and American readers because African readers where they exist at all are only interested in reading textbooks. I don't know if African writers always have a foreign audience in mind. What I do know is that they don't have to. At least I know that I don't have to. Last year the pattern of sales of Things Fall Apart in the cheap paperback edition was as follows: 800 copies in Britain, 20,000 in Nigeria; and about 2,500 in all other places.* (Achebe, 1975:43).

This cliché was again refuted by Adaobi Tricia Nwaubani in her *The Secret of Nigerian Book Sales*, where she recounted the story of a Nigerian bookseller,

> *who has been in the business since 1999, and says he cannot meet his customers' demands. [...] Wale Rasaki, the C.E.O. of Book Liquidator Ventures, has been selling thousands of second-hand books ... The most popular titles are books by John Grisham, Sidney Sheldon, Frederick Forsyth, Jackie Collins, Judith McNaught, Johanna Lindsey.* (Nwaubani, 2015).

Now, since African readers were consuming vast numbers of books from the West, does this imply that the West was writing for Africa? There is a more disturbing angle to this allegation. The arrogation of all the good things coming out of

Africa as being stirred up by outsiders, because nothing good was capable of coming from within, was a successful campaign that was initiated during the slavery period and consolidated during colonial times. According to it, the Dark Continent, as Africa was called then, was inherently bad, beyond redemption, or perhaps could only be redeemed with the aid of the white man. So arose the image of the white saviour, colonial masters who died on a cross while attempting to bring salvation to the poor condemned souls of the third world. Since this was a gospel that had been preached over and over again, it incarnated and became its own reality and self-verifiable truth. Even after colonisation had long ended, the damage had already been done. Africans found themselves respawning this myth, again and again, in different forms and shades. White is good, black is bad. Anything good happening in Africa must somehow have come from the West. Decolonisation is a long journey. So, in this light, we can understand how the current boom in African speculative fiction must somehow be connected to Western influence.

To understand the actual reason why genre fiction is now on the rise in Africa, we have to place African speculative fiction in the context of what is generally going on at the moment in the wider Africa literature scene as a whole. Because, at this time, African SFF fiction is booming, African literary fiction is again awakening from the coma it had been in after the era of Chinua Achebe, Wole Soyinka, Ngugi wa Thiong'o, and other writers of that generation. Writers like Chimamanda Adichie, Taiye Selasi, and Abubakar Adam Ibrahim are at the forefront of the literary genre. African literature is constantly winning and receiving nominations for major literary awards. This current gaining of prominence for the African literary genre concomitant with Africa SFF is no mere coincidence. It is the same force that is in operation. To make this clearer, we need to go back to when Anglophone African literature experienced its first international buzz.

Limitation of the Essay

The focus of this research is on the third wave of writing in Africa, which began as a result of European conquest. This wave of literature, as Gikandi noted, was "produced in the crucible of colonialism. ... the men and women who founded [...] modern African writing [...] were, without exception, products of the institutions that colonialism had introduced and developed in the continent." (Gikandi, 2004:379)".

It is pertinent to note that, prior to this, there were other waves of literature and storytelling in Africa in the written form. Gerard noted that the:

> *introduction of the writing skill to Africa was by no means a consequence of Western colonisation. [...] a substantial amount of poetry had been written in the Islamised areas of black Africa [...] And prior to that, the written art had been known and widely practised in [...] Ethiopia. European influence thus found its proper place in initiating the third phase in a historical process that has lasted for nearly 2,000 years.* (Gerard, 1993:24).

Most of the writings during these phases were lost but, judging from the fact that most of these writings took place when mythology played a significant part in the communities, chances are that there could have been a strong trend in speculative fiction during this era in Africa. However, our focus for this paper will be limited to the third phase of literacy in Africa; that is the period that began as a result of European conquest of Africa.

Literatures of Expectation: The Elephant in the Room

It was in the 1960's that Chinua Achebe published his ground-breaking novel, *Things Fall Apart*, and there was a buzz about African literature globally. Writers like Ngugi wa Thiong'o, Bessie Head, and Flora Nwakpa followed suit. The critics turned to them with a question. Now that African literature had emerged, what was the world's expectation of this tradition? Achebe opined that it was to educate and to fight the colonial system. He said:

> ... *it would be foolish to pretend that we have fully recovered from the traumatic effects of our first confrontation with Europe. Three or four weeks ago my wife, who teaches English in a boys' school, asked a pupil why he wrote about winter when he meant the harmattan. He said the other boys would call him a bushman if he did such a thing! [...] I think it is part of my business as a writer to teach that boy that there is nothing disgraceful about the African weather, that the palm-tree is a fit subject for poetry... I would be quite satisfied if my novels [...] did no more than teach my readers that their past—with all its imperfections—was not one long night of savagery from which the first Europeans acting on God's behalf delivered them.* (Achebe, 1975:44)

It wasn't only Achebe who held this view. According to Gikandi:

> *The heart of literary scholarship on the continent could not have acquired its current identity or function if the traumatic encounter between Africa and Europe had not taken place. Not only were the founders of modern Africa literature colonial subjects but colonialism*

was also to be the most important and enduring theme in their works. (Gikandi, 2004).

But, with time, as most African countries were gaining freedom and independence, the new emergent African leaders came with their own oppression. The focus of these writers turned to them. Wole Soyinka noted that, "The African writer needs an urgent release from the fascination of the past if he is to fulfil his function as the record of the mores and experience of his society and as the voice of vision in his own time" (1967, cited in Lindfors, 2008:26). Achebe, agreeing with Soyinka, noted that, "[...] One of the writer's main functions has always been to expose and attack injustice. Should we keep at the old theme of racial injustice (sore as it still is) when new injustices have sprouted all around us? I think not" (1964, cited in Lindfors 2008:26).

But whether it was to fight colonialism or to kick against the exploitation of African leaders on the continent, the general consensus among the pioneers of modern African literature was that the expectation of African literature was that it had to be political. Lindfors noted that,

> *the new literatures in English and French that have emerged in black Africa in the twentieth century have been profoundly influenced by politics. [...] Writers have served not only as chroniclers of contemporary political history but also as the advocates of radical social change. Their works thus both reflect and project the course of Africa's cultural revolution"* (2008:22).

Art for art's sake then is ideal for leisure, but not worthy of being engaged in by an Africa writer. Ngugi put it this way:

> *I looked forward to the day when all the preoccupation of African writers with colonial problems and politics would be over and we would all sit back and poke sophisticated irony at one another and laugh at ourselves… we would then indulge in the luxury of comedies of social manners…or explore the anguished world of lonely individuals abstracted from time and actual circumstances."* (2008:477).

For Brutus, to avoid this political stand is to produce unaesthetic artwork. He wrote,

> *An artist, a writer is a man who lives in a particular society and takes his images and ideas from that society. He must write about what he sees around him […] or he must come to terms with what is ugly in it and pretend that it is not there or that it is not bad. Having done that, he cuts himself off from large areas of experience, large areas of expression. This is the price he must pay because he has cut himself off from his fellow men.* (Brutus, 1976:100).

This stand and expectation was more concretised when Chinua Achebe became the editor of the Heinemann publishing company, which had a hand in the publication of the majority of literature published by the founders of modern African literature through the *African Writers Series*. Under his editorial, political literature became the only canon that he believed could serve as the framework for African writing. Those who wrote anything else were either not published or generally ignored by the critics if they ever succeeded in publishing it elsewhere. Some speculative fiction was published during this time but hardly made a wave like the way protest literature of its time had made an impact. Some of this SFF fiction could be seen in Mark Bould's essay, *African Science Fiction 101*.

This political expectation that was given to African literature was good in itself, but it also had a lot of pitfalls. Chief among these was that it constrained African literature from developing and growing into different sophisticated styles, themes, and genres. It is this precisely that held to ransom the sprouting of African speculative fiction. Writers wrote to fit into this political model so they could stand a chance of being published, to be taken as serious writers. Even when Ngugi wrote *Wizard of the Crow*, he was already an established protest fiction writer. The novel in itself was a political fantasy, so it perfectly fitted into this model. Literary fiction was the major output during this period because it easily suited the aim of political literature due to its direct style that mirrored real, societal life. Writing speculative fiction, especially of a type without any political intent, was viewed as some kind of frivolity reserved for the privilege of Western writers who weren't battling with the sort of political chaos being witnessed in Africa. For Achebe, such Western writers could engage in pure art; he was all for applied art and believed that this applied form of art should be the expectation of African literature. It was this background, established by the pioneers of modern African literature, that gave birth to the myth that Africans didn't write genre fiction because they had other social issues to bother them; a myth current African writers frown upon.

Articulating the damage done by this political model to the development of the whole body of African literature, Helen Andrews said that since *Things Fall Apart*, "the Anglophone African novel has, for the most part, remained as it was when Achebe launched it: unremarkable in its prose, flat in its characterization, anti-Western in its politics, and preoccupied with the confrontation between tradition and modernity" (see full quotation at the start of this paper).

This "protest" foundation was the cause for any writer working outside of this canon not being taken seriously. For instance, even with the major award won by Ben Okri's *Famished Road*, the work wasn't celebrated as much as it should have been in Nigeria because, unfortunately, it was a novel that didn't fit into the dominating framework which African literature was expected to fall into by those who had inaugurated it.

The Shift from Protest Literature: The Renaissance of African SFF

The shift began firstly with readers of African literature, when they began to snub it and move towards buying Western literature. Young African readers devoured science fiction, horror, and fantasy from the West. E. K. Mngodo (2017) recently commented in a blog that she wrote for the Caine Prize on how young African children she had met in Tanzania knew about Harry Potter but knew nothing about African writers from just a few miles away. One could argue that this is an infection of colonialism, a poison which causes one to cherish an outsider more than oneself. But, even if it could play a part here, I don't think that this is the main reason. Rather, it is the effect of making protest literature the default setting for African literature that has wreaked this damage, by causing a lack of diversity and not meeting the different tastes of individuals, who then sought to quench their thirst elsewhere. At some point, the majority of novels published by African writers became predictable. They were literally uninspired; political preaching masquerading as entertainment. For reading pleasure, particularly those who tended toward speculative fiction, African readers consequently turned to the West and Europe, since novels from African authors tended to be too serious, and offering no escape from the real world. These novels were published not for their aesthetic beauty but instead for their politically functionalistic stance.

Wole Soyinka also lamented the standard of this literature, especially from the *African Writer Series*, which was the dominant series during the 1960s, right through to the 1990s. This aforementioned series was responsible for the majority of published African novels at the time. With a loss of interest in indigenous literature, and readers migrating to Western works, combined with government censorship and cracking down on the publishing industry during the 1960s, the profit margin for the industry continued to fall to the point where many faced being unable to publish again. It didn't help that these companies refused to look within for the source of their problems. Readers were an easy scapegoat. "Africans only read textbooks" was the lame excuse publishers had for their failure. Thus, the stereotype of Africans not reading fiction only strengthened.

But the truth was, through their money, readers revolted and showed their power by putting an end to the excessive junking out of political treatise within the flesh of a novel. Even though it wasn't their function to write, the readers put to death the recycling of what they didn't want to see and paved the way for a revolution and the rise of SFF we are currently witnessing. With this recent shift, African lovers of literature began returning from the exile that their writers had sent them into. Although not all of them returned, African writers were now tasked with wooing them back. This too became the trend in the home movie industry, at a time when Western films were the dominant source of entertainment in Nigeria and most other parts of Africa. Through the ambition of the likes of Nollywood, with well-crafted scripts embracing the genre as a whole, horror and fantasy inclusive, it has become a force to reckon with, and the prime choice of entertainment on the continent.

It took African Writers a long time to break from this foundation. Even though, as readers, they enjoyed entertaining books which allowed them to easily escape from the world, as writers, they wanted to be taken seriously. This steered them towards political, and issues, writing. Ikhide R. Ikheloa (2017) often lamented how African writers poured all their continental frustrations into their stories. He wrote, "I have said that many African writers write poor fiction because they tend to force their anxieties about social conditions into the format of fiction. The result is often awkward; they should be writing essays."

After the death of Achebe, Andrews (2014) argued that his death would open up a new path for African literature. However, even before Achebe's death, African writers had begun an internal revolt which marked them as separate from this political trope. A major example in literary fiction was Adichie, whose work *Purple Hibiscus*, although set in a political atmosphere, managed to avoid these tropes in writing about a family fighting their own battle against an abusive father. In speculative fiction, Nnedi Okorafor led the way for young, ambitious African writers. It was, so to say, a herald signifying the new movement of African writers; those beyond the political trope who wanted, at the end of the day, to write what they enjoyed reading and didn't give a damn whether or not they would be taken as serious writers.

The Caine Prize played a role in this explosion of African SFF. Even though it wasn't the Caine Prize as such that began this revolution, it did became something of a platform for people who were tired of seeing issue-driven literature as being the sole representation of what African literature should be.

From its start up until present time, the Caine Prize remained a massive force and influence, because it is an award with the sole aim of unearthing fresh voices in African literature. It is huge in its power and ability to turn its winner and shortlisted writers from obscure entities into celebrities within African literature.

Two major revolts arose through the Caine Prize. One was led by Binyavanga Wainaina, known for being outspoken about neo-colonialism and gay rights. Wainaina expressed doubts about the colonial nature of the prize. Why should an award for African literature be hosted and presented in London? The second criticism, which is more pertinent to this essay, was about the kinds of stories being selected as winners. They were politically conscious stories, keeping in place the metaphysical foundation already established by Achebe's generation of writers. Some of the stories portrayed Africans as being poor due to the corruption of their leaders, police brutality, or the devastating effect of AIDS. Once again, these are stories where the artist seems to take their job too seriously: the job of being socially conscientious. These stories seemed to be making Africans out to be an NGO case. Some took to calling these stories poverty-porn literature.

Ikhide R. Ikheloa was critical of these stories being selected for the award. He wrote,

The Caine Prize for African Writing has been great for African

> *literature... The good news is that the Caine Prize is here to stay. The bad news is that someone is going to win the Caine Prize this year. [...] having read the stories on the shortlist I conclude that a successful African writer must be clinically depressed [...] the 2011 shortlist celebrate orthodoxy and mediocrity. They are a riot of exhausted clichés [...] Huts, moons, rapes, wars, and poverty. The monotony of misery simply overwhelms the reader.* (Ikehloa, 2011).

Habila articulated his own criticism thus:

> *I was at a Caine prize seminar a few years back and the discussion was on the state of the new fiction coming out of Africa. One of the panellists [...] accused the new writers of "performing Africa" for the world [...] but not in a real tragic sense, more in a [...] poverty-porn sense. [...] The result, for the reader ... [is] a sort of creeping horror that leads to a desensitisation to the reality being represented. The question to be asked then is whether this new writing [...] is just a "Caine-prize aesthetic"* (Habila, 2013).

The director of the prize later countered that nobody had set out with a template to select what sort of story should win the award; rather, it was from what was submitted that they simply chose the best.

It is not in our interests here to argue whether or not the Caine Prize was guilty as accused, but the merits of this indictment was that it opened up a major discussion and debate about what sorts of stories African writers were expected to write. Then, on the back of this criticism, there were outright calls for genre fiction and other sorts of stories. These suggestions resonated with many writers who had grown tired of protest-literature, but who were afraid of trying anything else for fear of it painting them as non-serious writers, or that there was no market for it. They saw in this the validity of something they had been toiling against alone, and encouraged them that they really were on the right path.

During this period, with the Caine Prize and all of its attendant criticisms, there were exuberant productions of distinctive kinds of stories, with various writers trying their hand at the sort of speculative fiction they enjoyed but had been tamed into veering away from. There were different anthologies that tried to showcase that Africans had other kinds of stories to tell, apart from one dimensional protest literature. Ivor Hartmann created his anthology *AfroSF*, which was the first modern African science fiction anthology. Other speculative fiction anthologies followed suit, and literary magazines, like *Omenana*, were formed to cater for the needs of African writers of genre fiction. Individual writers began sending their speculative fiction out beyond Africa and were getting published. Geoff Ryman, a Canadian, would later found the *African Speculative Fiction Society*, which had an annual award for genre fiction from African writers. He also formed a Facebook group dedicated to African SFF which, at the time of writing, had over a thousand members. Wole Talabi began documenting lists of published African speculative fiction. Each day sees an exponential growth of this list.

There was again an awakening to the world of African writers who had previously created speculative fiction which the rest of the world knew little about because of the shadow that had been cast by the metaphysical foundation of African literature being only political. In light of this, we can understand the air of surprise as noted by Onwualu, where people began to discuss African speculative fiction and were increasingly excited by what they were discovering.

Dangers of Expectation/Conclusion

Will the current rise in African speculative fiction endure for a long time? I had hoped it would be so. However, there is a possibility that what happened so long ago to African literature, when Achebe and co. started, could reoccur. This could easily happen if the practitioners of this genre become fixated on a single theme or style. Inventiveness and risk-taking are what advance art. The horror genre became a victim of this in the West when it became obsessed with slasher tropes. As a result, its audience dwindled. Recently, it has made a comeback, mostly through genre-blending, with many of its current consumers viewing it as a psychological thriller with supernatural elements. If African speculative writers can avoid definition and a dogmatic expectation of what the genre should offer to the world, and remains open to all the possibilities therein, its place in world literature is secured.

Work Cited

Achebe, C., 1975. *Morning Yet on Creation Day: Essays*. London: Heinemann.

Andrews, H., 2014. *Up From Colonialism*. [online] Available through: <http://www.claremont.org/crb/article/up-from-colonialism/> [Accessed 1 September 2017].

Bould, M., 2017. African Science Fiction 101. *SFRA Review*. [e-journal] 311 Winter, pp. 11-18. Available through: <http://sfra.org/resources/sfra-review/311.pdf> [Accessed 15 August 2017].

Brutus, D. 1976. Protest Against Apartheid. In D. Duerden and C. Pieterse (eds). *Protest and Conflict*. London: Heinemann Publishers.

Gerard, A. S., 1993. Sub-Saharan Africa's Literary History in a Nutshell. In C. F. Swanepoel (ed.). *Comparative Literature and African Literature*. Pretoria: Via Afrika.

Gikandi, S., 2004. Africa literature and the Colonial Factor. In I. Abiloa and S. Gikandi (eds.). *The Cambridge History of African and Caribbean Literature*, Vol. 1. Cambridge: Cambridge University Press.

Habila, H., 2013. We Need New Names by NoViolet Bulawayo – review. *The Guardian*. [online] Available through: <https://www.theguardian.com/books/2013/jun/20/need-new-names-bulawayo-review> [Accessed 10 September 2017].

Ikheloa, R. I., 2011. The 2011 Caine Prize: How Not to Write About Africa. *xokigbo.com*. [online] Available through: <https://xokigbo.com/2012/03/11/the-2011-caine-prize-how-not-to-write-about-africa/> [Accessed 10 September 2017].

Ikheloa, R. I., 2017. Chinua Achebe and contemporary African literature. *xokigbo.com*. [online] Available through: <https://xokigbo.com/2017/05/06/chinua-achebe-and-contemporary-african-literature/> [Accessed 10 September 2017].

Lindfors, B., 1979. Politics, Culture, and Literary Form. In T. Olaniyan. and A. Quayson (eds.) 2008. *Africa Literature: An Anthology of Criticism and Theory*. Victoria: Blackwell.

Mngodo, E. K., 2017. Raising the Next Generation of African Writers. *caineprize.com*. [online] Available through: <http://caineprize.com/blog/2017/8/17/raising-the-next-generation-of-african-writers-by-esther-karin-mngodo> [Accessed 1 September 2017].

Nwaubani, T. A., 2015. The Secret of Nigerian Book Sales. *newyorker.com*. [online] Available through: <https://www.newyorker.com/business/currency/the-secret-of-nigerian-book-sales> [Accessed 1 September 2017].

Onwualu, C., 2016. Emerging Trends in African Speculative Fiction. *strangehorizons.com*. [online] Available through: <http://strangehorizons.com/non-fiction/columns/emerging-trends-in-african-speculative-fiction/> [Accessed 9 August 2017].

Ryman, G., 2017. 21 Today: The Rise of Speculative Fiction, year by year. *The Manchester Review*. 1ssue 18. Available through: <http://www.themanchesterreview.co.uk/?p=8006> [Accessed 25 July 2017].

Thiong'O, N. W., 2008. Writers in Politics: The Power of Words and the Words of Power. In T. Olaniyan and A. Quayson (eds.) 2008. *Africa Literature: An Anthology of Criticism and Theory*. Victoria: Blackwell Publishing.

Scientists in Nigerian Science Fiction

By Polina Levontin

Science fiction is a recent genre classification in Nigerian literature. The standard references such as The Cambridge Companion to Science Fiction (2003) or Palgrave Histories of Literature: The history of science fiction (2005) are yet to mention Nigerian writers. Currently, there is only a limited body of work available in English, but it has been growing steadily since 2000. African literature tends to be analysed from the perspectives of race and ethnicity, (post)colonialism and globalisation. However, I am more interested in the role that science-fiction could play in the conversation about science and scientists. Canonical works from North American and European authors have been considered in this way, but to my knowledge little has been done to interrogate the narratives around science in Nigerian literature. This study examines representations of scientists in Nigerian science fiction in relation to discourses on gender, science and technology.

There is sufficient evidence for the idea that fictional representations and public opinion of science are linked, and that studying representations of scientists is relevant to the task of understanding public perceptions. These linkages are not yet well understood however, and care must be taken in proposing social implications of fictional representations without further research. The evidence points to a complex relationship which is mediated by journalists and policy makers, and is contingent on individually held values. The relationship between Nigerian science fiction and the Nigerian public's attitudes to science is even more uncertain, because domestic markets are nascent and the majority of readers of Nigerian science fiction are in the Global North. Although it would be premature to draw conclusions about the Nigerian public's attitudes to science based on these texts, this study identifies socially relevant hypotheses that could be explored in further research.

Introduction

It is not widely known that Nigerian science fiction (Nigerian SF) exists, and so one of the first tasks is to identify a corresponding body of literature. This requires qualifying the terms 'Nigerian' and 'science fiction'. For this study, the term 'Nigerian' refers to the author and includes both residents of Nigeria and members of the diaspora. Definitions of an 'African writer' vary and are contested.[1] None of the writers considered here would be excluded by the definition of an 'African writer' used in the Caine Prize[2], a major literary award:

> 'An African writer' is taken to mean someone who was born in Africa, or who is a national of an African country, or who has a parent who is African by birth or nationality.

All the authors discussed are either Nigerian citizens or first-generation Nigerians living in the diaspora who maintain links with Nigerian cultural life.

For the second term, 'science fiction', I am relying on the publishing industry's definition, using those literary sources that are marketed as 'science fiction'. Comic books, graphic novels, art, film or science fiction sources in the media other than the written word are not considered. The immediate consequence of defining Nigerian SF in this way is to narrow a list of eligible publications, enabling a survey of a large

---

1. Who is African? *African Speculative Fiction Society.* [online] Available at: <http://www.africansfs.com/african> [Accessed 30 November 2017].
2. Caine Prize, eligibility. *cainprize.com.* [online] Available at: <http://caineprize.com/how-to-enter/> [Accessed 30 November 2017].

proportion of relevant works, both in paper and purely digital formats.

Why study representations of scientists?

Representations of scientists in fiction and film are of interest in their own right, as components of literature. However, research into representations of science and scientists may be motivated by policy questions. One of the common assumptions is the existence of a strong link between the fictional representations of scientists and the ideas about science held by the public. A corollary to this assumption is a belief that public mistrust of science is driven by fiction.

How do representations influence the public?

Researchers generally agree that fictional representations can draw critical attention to issues that are neglected in society. For example, Kitzinger meta-analysis reveals a tendency of science fiction to foreground 'questions of distribution, democracy and accountability' (2009), and to highlight unpredictability of research, producing scenarios where control of science and technology is elusive. In explaining a motivation for her seminal study, *From Faust to Strangelove: representations of the Scientist in Western Literature*, Roslynn D. Haynes offers the view that 'writers are reflecting more or less faithfully the attitudes of their society towards actual science and scientists' (1994:5). The claim that fiction reflects public perception of science is less controversial than the theory that literary fiction is capable of reshaping public attitudes, though some studies corroborate this. For example, Barnett et al.

(2006) offer empirical evidence that fictional representations might indeed influence public understanding negatively, from a perspective of science communication. They demonstrated how exposure to a geologically themed science fiction film worsened students' understanding of the subject, by blurring the line between fiction and fact. The impact of fictional narratives, they suggest, is particularly strong in cases where events cannot be witnessed in reality, as with dinosaurs of the past or global catastrophic climate change of the future.

Sources and methodology

Looking at a large number of texts simultaneously necessitates a *distant reading* (Moretti, 2007) approach with a focus on patterns rather than individual characters. The aim is to characterise and describe thematically a variety of scientist characters in Nigerian SF.

The majority of the scientists came from short stories, a few from novellas, such as "Proposition 23" (2012) and "An Indigo Song for Paradise" (2015), both by Efe Okogu. I was able to find only four relevant novels: *Lagoon* (2014) and *The Book of Phoenix* (2015) by Nnedi Okorafor, *Nigerians in Space* (2014) by Deji Olukotun, and *Rosewater* (2016b) by Tade Thompson. Other print sources comprise five collections of short stories and novellas: *AfroSF* (2012), *AfroSF2* (2015), *Terra Incognita* (2015) – containing both Nigerian and other African writers, and *Lagos_2060* (2013) and *How to Spell Naija in 100 Short Stories* (2016) that are solely Nigerian.

Deji Olukotun (USA), Nnedi Okorafor (USA), Efe Okogu (Mexico), and Tade Thompson (UK) live in the diaspora. Because these writers publish outside Nigeria, reviews of their work are more readily available in the UK. All of the original texts are at the moment of writing available in print or online. Further, the complete database of characters discussed in this study is available online[3], through GitHub, along with the code for the statistical analysis.

Analysis of scientist characters

Field of research

Most scientist characters in Nigerian SF are identified with a specific field of research (Figure 1). The scientist characters are divided into eight academic fields: robotics, environmental science, genetics, medicine, virology, energy, engineering, and space-time (Figure 1). These categories are selected to capture the diversity of scientists in specific enough detail, without creating too many subgroups. Space-time is the most popular specialisation (Figure 1).

The focus on area of expertise and gender is the basis for the analysis of representations of scientists in Western literature, where Haynes (1994, 2016) shows that specialisation and gender correlate with fictional representation patterns. Looking at a historical dimension in Western literature, natural scientists tended to be 'complimentary to the point of eulogy' in the 19th century and commonly afterwards (Haynes 1994:109). After the Second World War the portraits of physicists, biologists and chemists became tainted due to association with military uses, such as nuclear, biological

---

3. Representation of scientists in Nigerian science-fiction. *github.com*. [online] Available at: <https://github.com/pl202/NigerianSF> [Accessed on 30 November 2017].

and chemical weapons, while the portraits of astronomers remained largely positive (Haynes 1994:276).

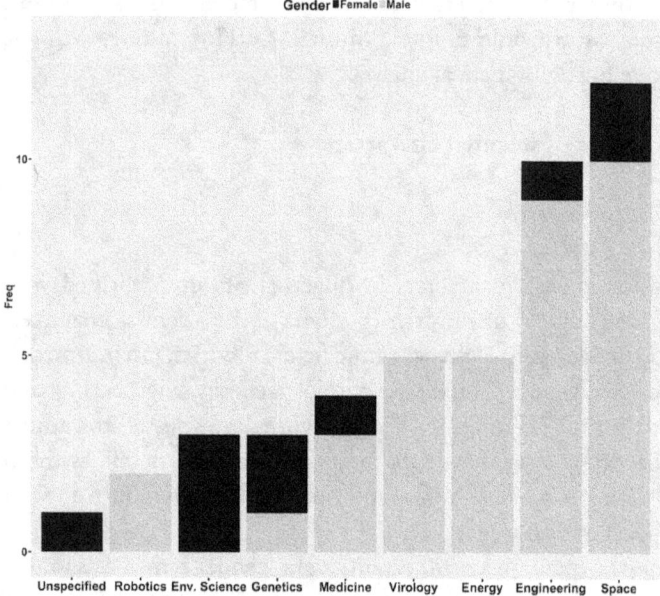

Figure 1 helps examine the data in terms of the scientists' gender and area of expertise.

Female scientists

One of the first things which stands out from the data is the gender imbalance (Figure 1). Women are underrepresented both amongst the authors and the scientist characters. Out of the 43 scientist characters, only 9 are female, of which 4 are the protagonist or a major character. Female Nigerian SF writers are also a minority. Cross-referencing the gender of the characters with the gender of the authors, it appears that female writers are more likely to have female scientist characters in their fiction. Albeit, even amongst the scientist characters written by women, less than half are female scientists. Male Nigerian SF authors overwhelmingly imagine scientists as male. Female authors were also found to be more likely to depict women as scientists in Western SF (Merrick, 2012).

About half of the female scientists are part of a romance narrative, involving courtship or early stages of marriage. All female scientists are described as physically attractive. At some point in all of the narratives containing a female scientist, she appears as a young woman - whereas the majority of male scientists are presented as middle-aged (Figure 2).

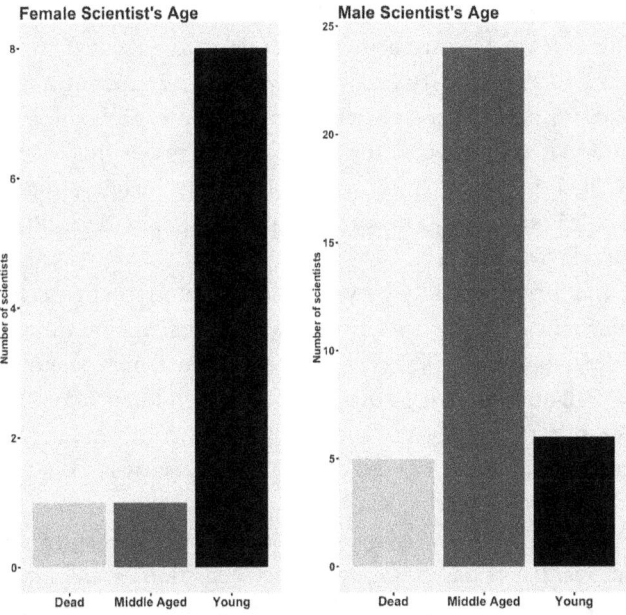

Figure 2. Age composition of characters, by gender.

So indispensable is appearance for female scientists in Nigerian SF that there is even a character who turns to science solely out of fear of losing her legendary beauty. Evelyn McDuffie ("Deletion", Nwonwu, 2013b) discovers a way to prolong youth, but her achievement is stigmatised: she amasses a business empire that turns politically corrupt, and her research is rumoured to be linked to a new and deadly virus that starts to decimate the population.

One of the female characters – Rekia ("Mango Republic", Agbedeh, 2013) - is a scientist, but her research is so marginal to the story there is no hint of what she does. Instead, the story focuses on her role as the wife of the protagonist Aromire, and as a mother-to-be of his child. By contrast, Aromire's many achievements as a scientist are named and valorised. Rekia suffers seven miscarriages while working as a scientist; she pleads for her husband's permission to leave work, because the doctor has assured her that she will succeed in carrying to term only if she becomes a housewife. This story imagines that in 2060 it is still the norm for all important family decisions to be made by men.

The incompatibility between the goal of motherhood and aspirations of being a scientist is a persistent theme through all the narratives in Nigerian SF. Out of nine female scientists, only Adaora (*Lagoon*, Okorafor, 2014) has children, and as the novel progresses they are taken away from her by her husband as a matter of safety – success in her role as a scientist coincides with failure to protect her children.

Bumi's (*The Book of Phoenix*, Okorafor, 2015) monstrousness as a scientist is based largely on her depiction as an abusive mother to an orphan girl, Phoenix, whom Bumi helps to genetically engineer. Bumi abuses Phoenix both physically and psychologically, subjecting her to painful experiments. Phoenix escapes the 'secure' American government laboratory, but her childhood trauma makes her an uncontrollable, apocalyptic weapon.

Many male scientists in Nigerian SF have children, and the conflict between their careers and fatherhood is not explicitly part of any narrative. When Wale Olufumni, in *Nigerians in Space* (Olukotun, 2014), goes into exile, hiding from government-backed gangsters, he still gets to raise his son Dayo (after kidnapping him from his mother).

Nevertheless, most of the female scientists possess inspiring character features. Adaora, in particular, is smart, brave and independent – a woman who stands up to her husband, the army, the president, the church and even the aliens. DevilDog defies the establishment, Oyin Da - the government, Violet defies a corporation, while Tara helps brings a corporation down.

However, these characters don't feel particularly committed to science – nearly half of the female scientists quit science in the various narratives.

Women and 'Mother Nature'

Three of the female scientists are identified with nature through their work in the field of environmental science [Adaora, Yinka ("Animals on the Run", Egboluche, 2013), Tara], as women are associated with 'mother nature' in many cultures. In fact, there are no male scientists in the field – Wale Olufumni is a geologist, but he is a lunar geologist and his scientific interests are mostly to do with space exploration.

So, while female scientists protect nature, prolong beauty,

give birth and get married, male scientists conjure new ways to produce energy, build robots and invent space-time travel (Figure 1).

Scientists and power

Scientists' research in Nigerian SF is always politicised, especially in the areas of energy, genetics and robotics. This is likely due to the heightened attention in Nigeria to oil, ethnicity and unemployment. Nigeria, which had 45 million people at independence in 1960, has approximately 190 million people at time of writing and is projected to grow to 400 million by 2050 to become the world's third most populous country, after India and China. It is not surprising then that Nigerian SF writers are anxious about governing the country in a future that is under threat from climate change, regionalism and technologies which eliminate jobs while the population grows rapidly. Nigeria as a state is a product of colonialism, and is still working to resolve the tensions amongst groups that coexist uneasily within its borders (Bourne, 2015).

Scientists in Nigerian SF are frequently presented as well intentioned, but their efforts are compromised by the system. The scientists are often left without agency or control over their inventions – in Nigerian SF, they are frequently victimised. The governments have the prime responsibility for mostly dystopian futures depicted in this fiction, except in the "Amphibian Attack" (Ashiru, 2013) and 'Lagoon' narratives, where elected politicians are outwitted and overpowered by corporations and aliens, respectively.

These powers are corrupting or derailing science in almost every example of Nigerian SF, and nowhere is the pessimism over science's ability to deliver 'progress' expressed more directly than in *The Book of Phoenix*, where the protagonist Phoenix justifies destroying all the centres of science, housed in in seven towers located all over the world, with the scientists still in them:

> *Behind the good intentions and amazing science, however, was abomination. Weapons, the quest for immortality, how far could we go... The foundation of all the towers was always always always corrupt, driven by a lusty greed.*
>
> *To kill a snake, cut off the head.*
> (Okorafor, 2015:98)

Genetics

There are perhaps too few geneticists in the sample to make generalisations, but genetic manipulation is associated with the most objectionable research and characters. One of the three geneticists, Violet in "CJ" (Chinelo, 2015), quits science rather than pursuing unethical research; she trades 'unnatural' biogenetics for 'natural' farming:

> *Anyway, the company wants to figure out a way to track and identify these people [with super human abilities], and they want to use our bio-genetic research to do it. Well, I told them to go fuck themselves, so they put me on indefinite suspension. With pay, of course. Ola and I bought the Yangs' old farm. (Terra Incognita, 2015:177)*

Bumi, in *The Book of Phoenix*, uses genetic research to track and identify humans with special abilities, and so does Mathew Halliday in "Ofe!" (Aliyu, 2012) - this is a strange coincidence. Surveillance is a strong theme in all three plots involving geneticists in Nigerian SF. In *The Book of Phoenix* it is not just Bumi who is trying to keep track of her creation, it is 'All of THEM, the "Big Eye" – the Tower 7 scientists, lab assistants, lab technicians, doctors, administrative workers, guards, and police.' Phoenix, who was genetically engineered in Tower 7, recounts that everyone who worked in the tower watched the 'speciMen' all the time. Their attempted total surveillance and control inevitably failed, but their complicity justified their total extermination, in the mind of Phoenix.

In "Ofe!", another geneticist, Mathew Halliday, is willing to conduct gruesome experiments on living human beings and has used his research to survey the entire population of West Africa and identify 13 individuals carrying alien genes that endow them with superhuman abilities. He manages to trap them in order to experiment on them, but they fight back and escape.

These similarities in the plots must speak to specific fears about genetics as knowledge that enables discrimination against people based on their genetic makeup, rather than on the basis of their character or actions. In Nigerian SF, genetics research is associated with enabling the government with new technologies of control and surveillance.

Robotics and unemployment

Robotics, like genetics, are the kinds of technologies that are associated with surveillance. In Nigerian SF too, we find many instances of various types of drones snooping and relaying information to governments. However, we don't find the scientists preoccupied with developing robotics for this purpose. They are developing robots to replace people, making humans superfluous as labourers, and as lovers. Although robots are nearly ubiquitous in Nigerian SF, there are only two scientists which predominantly build robots, both found in the *Lagos_2060* collection of short stories. Abdul Rahman, in "Metal Feet" (Olofinlua, 2013), builds a gynoid to replace his wife. She narrates the story in the second person, depicting not just the break-up of her marriage but social devastation brought on by robots:

> *As you step out of the train, you see the huge TV-billboard-screen, tuned to NN24. You listen to the headlines: Couple Married by a Robot in Ikeja. You see a smiling couple with a robot Priest. Protests in Seven Cities of Lagos Over the Introduction of Robot Teachers into the Education System. You see images of people in protest on the huge screen. You see the shields pushing them back from approaching the state house; you stare at the police, wonder if they cannot feel the plight of the majority. Then you stare at their feet. Cold metal. (Lagos_2060,* 2013:209)

Abdul is not a rogue, evil scientist. He only conforms to the dominant narrative of his society that values robots more than humans. The story "Animals on the Run" (Egboluche, 2013) has similarly dark visions of robots displacing humans. The scientist creating robots in that story is Julio Akanchawa, who is regarded as a genius worldwide and is admired in Nigeria for his technological inventions by all except his girlfriend Yinka, and her father. "Animals on the Run" is a conservative narrative in many respects, suspicious not just of technological, but also of social changes, such as the emancipation of women. Yinka, for instance, is admiringly described as superior to other 'insolent and bossy' contemporary women: 'Yinka was different. She had a good job [an ecologist], she was well paid but chose to be submissive to him [Julio]' (55). Yinka thinks Julio's research is harmful, but does not confront him directly. Instead, she writes an online journalistic column that Julio reads and makes anonymous defensive remarks in the comments section. It gives the story a satirical edge. In her blog, Yinka connects robotics to both social and environmental problems, blaming mechanisation in the agricultural North of Nigeria for unsustainable migration to Lagos:

> *People also came from the North, the very rich north currently enjoying mechanized agriculture courtesy of robotics. Many lost their jobs because the robots did the farming. [...] I wonder why government establishments would use robots when people still need jobs. Is this an achievement?* (*Lagos_2060*, 2013:59)

We learn that, although the use of robotics in agriculture increased productivity, the beneficiaries were mostly foreign investors who bought the land. Yinka's father is one of the Nigerian landowners who was forced to sell his farm, but those who lost the most were the low-skilled agricultural labourers. Yinka's father holds Julio personally responsible, therefore withholding his consent to the marriage. Julio tries to defend himself, saying to Yinka's father: 'Baba, I was trained to be a robotic scientist, I do what I do to make life better... to uplift mankind, to provide easier ways of doing things.' (62) Julio loses this argument, relents, abandons robotics, and is given an opportunity to lead the new government's efforts towards socially and environmentally sustainable development. The story gives no clue as to how the very real problems of an increasing population can be reconciled with an increasing productivity of labour brought about by mechanisation (which enables fewer people to accomplish the same amount of work).

It is not the only Nigerian SF narrative to focus on the issue of a superfluous labour force, and to discuss solutions such as the Universal Basic Income (UBI), critically. Two main problems are highlighted. First, the scheme will be open to manipulation by those in power, giving it extra tools to suppress dissent or exclude those outside state control. In "Animals on the Run", those living outside the state of Lagos are excluded from UBI; in "Proposition 23", those showing the slightest potential for political dissent are cut off from state assistance. The second problem is the purported moral damage. Yinka's conservative father, a character representing traditional Nigerian values in "Animals on the Run" purports that UBI is damaging to character: 'our youths have become lazy because they are paid even when they don't work.' (60). In "Mango Republic", the state only undertakes to support through UBI those who desire to work, while the citizens deemed 'lazy' are expelled from the city. As in "Proposition 23", being excluded from the state-controlled welfare system means almost certain death, as both stories are set in a post-apocalyptic environment where nature has turned inhospitable to human survival.

There are hints that some universal welfare systems work well in "CJ", where Violet is suspended indefinitely with pay from her work after she complains that she finds her genetics research project unethical. In that vision of the Nigerian future, no one seems to be having economic problems – the central conflict in "CJ" is about homosexuality.

Energy and the failure of progress

Working on developing alternative sources of energy invariably leads to tragedy for scientists in Nigerian SF. The country's crippling dependence on oil does not end happily as alternative sources of energy are invented. An unnamed scientist in "An Indigo Song for Paradise" (Okogu, 2015), announcing free and unlimited source of energy, declares hopefully:

> *This is the end of all our problems,' a man was saying loudly to a group of listeners. 'With free energy finally within our grasp, we will easily tackle all other problems facing society. […] I predict a great change in society, ladies and gentlemen, now that we have crossed this scientific thresh-hold. In fact, I will go so far as to say today heralds the end of wars and all forms of crime and violence. […] With the end of war, comes the end of the economy. No more shall he con me, that masked devil known as capitalism. No longer!* (*AfroSF2*, 2015:437)

No sooner has he finished his speech than an armed gang bursts into the conference, killing the speaker, and turning the university into a war zone. In fact, the whole city succumbs to an apocalypse shortly after.

Both scientists working on alternative energy sources in *Nigerians in Space* are murdered by the corrupt government outfit whose power is welded to oil-dependence.

In the two remaining narratives featuring energy scientists, the invention of cheap energy alternatives to oil leads to the break-up of Nigeria, with dire consequences outside of Lagos. Ravi Shukhavati, in "Cold Fusion" (Arigbabu, 2013), figures out how to produce energy cheaply. The Lagos State Government acquires rights to the technology, enriching itself and seeking to rule the rest of Nigeria, nearly sparking another war between regions. The scientist himself does not fare well – he is pursued for his knowledge by assassins and kidnappers. We learn that he has gone into hiding and lives in constant fear.

In "Coming Home" (Falade, 2013), Lagos gets its energy from a new form of nuclear power, secedes from the rest of Nigeria, and becomes a rich but repressive regime, instating public executions for minor offences. Dr Martin – one of the members of the Lagosian scientific establishment – supports such measures, explaining to his estranged daughter, who is visiting from New York, that such death penalties have been effective in rooting out corruption in Lagos. On their first outing together, they are planning to witness an execution of a government official accused of stealing from a budget allocated for improving science laboratories in schools – it is unclear if the author is critical.

Medicine and engineering

The majority of scientists in Nigerian SF are driven by a utopian impulse but almost never does their research actually benefit humanity. Medical scientists are either murdered by the state, which resists modernisation, like Mohamed Farai in *Nigerians in Space*, or have their research subverted by powerful interests in a way that makes humanity distinctly worse off. For example, an unnamed scientist in "Annihilation" (Nwonwu, 2013a) creates a cure for cancer, but instead of lifting the burden of a disease his invention leads to a widespread drug epidemic and, even more devastating to society, a 'war on drugs'. Evelyn McDuffie's medical breakthrough on prolonging youth and increasing longevity creates stark social divisions between those who can afford the medical treatment and those who cannot.

Engineers have a greater variety of fates than any other category of fictional scientists in Nigerian SF. These range from "Budo", who develops weapons to fight off colonialists in 18th century Nigeria, in an alternative history narrative by Tade Thompson (2016b podcast), to Dayo Olufumni in *Nigerians in Space*, who engineers a lamp which imitates moonlight – an invention ignored by everyone except captive abalone. Occasionally, engineers are shown to create beautiful but ethereal things. Deph, in "An Indigo Song for Paradise", makes a magnificent pair of wings but they get ripped apart by gangster's bullets moments after the first flight.

Engineers also feature within a survivalist narrative, where humans cling to existence through heavy reliance on technology in a world made uninhabitable through ecological disaster. Such a setting, where Lagos is a tightly regulated techno-bubble in a post-apocalyptic Nigeria, is the premise of Okogu's "Proposition 23" in *AfroSF* and "Mango Republic". "Mango Republic" is more enthusiastic about technology than all other narratives. It is nature that is presented as a threat. Engineers and other scientists working for government institutions are actually making life better for the remaining inhabitants in a post-apocalyptic world. The city is designed to be sustainable and self-sufficient. There are city farms, recycling, renewable energy, waste treatment, artificial weather, and a healthy populace. In "Mango Republic", engineers are the government, which is led by Aremu Adigun – himself a scientist with three PhDs. This relative prosperity has a price – freedom. Population is controlled by limiting the number of children to two. Lagos is protected against immigrants by a wall – it has become 'the most beautiful prison in the world ever conceived by man', (197). Within the walls, people's lives are watched and regulated by engineers – people have become parts of a machine called Lagos that is ran from the Lagos

Institute of Science and Technology (LIST). But, with nature turned into the enemy of mankind, Lagos is seen as the best alternative – it is the number one destination, the new Rome:

> *There had been a lot of scientific research spearheaded by the LIST, which had made Lagos a Mecca of innovations and all roads led here.* (*Lagos_2060*, 2013:197)

Space Time Travel

Governments are the main problem for scientists in Nigerian SF who want to travel to a different time or universe. Several are imprisoned, interrogated, tortured and killed by fictional Nigerian governments: Wale Olufumni, Dr. Emalaba, Dr. Kehinde Abaseki, and Prof. Aloy Ogene. With the exceptions of Tade thompson's *The Bicycle Girl* (2014) and a follow-up novel, *Rosewater* (2016b), those who discover time travel don't actually get to undertake the journey. Not all scientists want to: Dr. Ngozi ("A Starlit Night", Akib, 2013), who discovers time travel by accident, working on herbs, thinks it is a dangerous type of knowledge and tries to hide it. When it is stolen, Dr. Ngozi dies of heartbreak and anxiety.

Virology

The field of virology has both the scientists who make viruses and those who fight them. Dr. Chris Yadua ("Deletion") creates a cure for the deletion-virus, working secretly from the government which seems to condone the epidemic. De Sampa ('Minority Report', Nwokolo, 2016) is a virologist whom the world only recognises as a priest – for many decades he uses his scientific knowledge to exercise power over a rural community. When he dies, the virus escapes and spreads to become an epidemic. Dr. Dafe and Dr. Duke put a stop to it, but no one believes them when they claim the virus was engineered by De Sampa. Another virologist, Mr. Adam ("Notes from Gethsemane", Thompson, 2012), creates a virus targeting an invasive alien entity. Virologists, in the sampled Nigerian SF stories, are all discussed in the context of biological weapons. Interestingly, they are all dealing with viruses that are engineered rather than naturally occurring.

Discussion

Mark Bould criticises literary scholars of African fiction for deploying a 'de-science fictionalized discourse' which treats 'anything irreal as some kind of postcolonial magic realism or avant-gardist experimentalism' (2015). He asserts that science fiction in Africa is at least a century old, and gives examples of many African novels which could be read as science fiction but were appropriated by postcolonial theory while ignoring their 'sf structures and moments'. Frelik mentions a possibility that these various 'previously unnoticed or unrecognised' texts that were first approached within the framework of post-colonialism will be reabsorbed into SF – 'discovered and brought into its fold.' (2015:280-284).

The reluctance to label African stories as science fiction is a legacy of a colonializing discourse. It is part of the discourse which upholds the hegemony of Western knowledge over African systems of enquiry (Mbembe, 2015). Suppressing the history of African science is a precursor to not recognising African stories as science fiction. Viewed from a Eurocentric position, the history of science fiction appears rooted in Europe, which is presented as both the centre and the origin of this literary mode (Roberts, 2005) – a tree, on which African science fiction is depicted as the newest branch. Academic research tends to compare African science fiction to Western literary cannon. This puts African science fiction at risk of being seen as derivative: imitating Western forms, or transplanting Western narratives into new 'exotic' African settings. Thus, the Efe Okogu novella "Proposition 23" is said to reinterpret Gibson's *Neuromancer* (Omelsky, 2014). Omelsky, who is clearly an enthusiast of African science fiction, still writes the following, very problematic generalisation:

> *These works are not innovative in the broader science fiction context. They recycle many of the existing tropes and conventions of Euro-American SF and insert them into distinctly African cultural geographies.* (Omelsky, 2014:38)

Conclusion

Unavoidably, the perception of patterns in literature is influenced by the cultural position and the knowledge base of the critical scholar. For example, a prevalent of Nigerian history predisposes a reader to imagine that Nigerian SF is preoccupied with corrupt and inadequate governments. Would a Nigerian reader, too, see the failure of the scientists to improve human condition as the consequence of bad governance and conclude that the writers are reflecting a mood of political pessimism in Nigeria? Is the approach to gender in this study Eurocentric?

When compared to reality, science fiction offers a more progressive view of gender in science, in both Nigerian and Western fiction. But, whereas Western SF is approaching gender equality in depicting scientists, Nigerian SF is lagging behind (taking the normative view that gender equality is ideal). The lack of fictional role models may hamper efforts to inspire the next generation of female scientists and engineers (Merrick, 2012).

One of the overarching themes in Nigerian SF is the inadequacy of science and scientists, whose efforts often result in unintended negative consequences for society; and death, infamy, torture and persecution of the scientists themselves. This pessimism raises important policy questions. What governance structures need to be in place to make sure that good inventions are not misused? How does a society ensure that scientific research is conducted on ethical grounds? How can Nigeria decolonize its academy and rehabilitate the status of historically locally produced knowledge? What can be done to limit the impact of technology, especially robotics, on unemployment? If fiction correctly reflects public pessimism with respect to genetics research, what has gone wrong and how should the scientific community or the government respond?

This study focused on fictional scientists in Nigerian SF, assuming that their representations could offer insights of attitudes towards science. This particular frame of enquiry directed away from analysis of the literary qualities of texts. A close analysis of individual works was sacrificed in order to produce an overview in an attempt to discover qualities shared by many texts. Hopefully, there will be interest amongst other researchers to follow up on some of the themes highlighted, with a closer look at individual works of Nigerian SF. As Nigerian SF is a rapidly growing field, I particularly hope that my findings with respect to gender will soon be out of date.

Cited Works

Barnett, M., Wagner, H., Gatling, A., Anderson, J., Houle, M. and Kafka, A., 2006. Impact of science fiction film on student understanding of science. *Journal of Science Education and Technology*, 15(2), pp. 179-191.

Bould, M., 2015. *African Science Fiction 101: Update 2*, December. [online]. Available through: <https://markbould.com/2015/12/12/african-science-fiction-101-update-2/> [Accessed 30 November 2017].

Bourne, R., 2015. *Nigeria: A new history of a turbulent century*. Zed Books.

Egboluche, O., 2013. Animals on the Run. *Lagos_2060: exciting sci-fi stories from Nigeria*. DADA books.

Falade, R., 2013. Coming Home. *Lagos_2060: exciting sci-fi stories from Nigeria*. DADA books.

Frelik, P., 2015. Postcolonialism and Science Fiction by Jessica Langer (review). *Science Fiction Film and Television*, 8(2): 280-284.

Haynes, R., 1994. *From Faust to Strangelove: representations of the Scientist in Western Literature*. The John Hopkins University Press.

Haynes, R., 2016. Whatever happened to the 'mad, bad' scientist? Overturning the stereotype. *Public Understanding of Science*. 25(1): 31-44.

James, E. and Mendelsohn, F., (eds), 2003. *The Cambridge companion to science fiction*. Cambridge University Press.

Kitzinger, J., 2009. Questioning the sci-fi alibi: a critique of how 'science fiction fears' are used to explain away public concerns about risk. *Journal of Risk Research*, 13(1): 73-86.

Mbembe, A., 2015. Decolonizing knowledge and the question of the archive. An Africa is a Country Ebook. *Africa is a Country* [online]. Available at: <https://africaisacountry.atavist.com/decolonizing-knowledge-and-the-

question-of-the-archive> [Accessed 30 November 2017].

Merrick, H., 2012. Challenging implicit gender bias in science: positive representations of female scientists in fiction. *Jurnalul Practicilor Comunitare Pozitive*, 4.

Moretti, F., 2007. *Graphs, Maps, Trees: Abstract Models for Literary History*. Verso.

Nwokolo, C., 2016. The Minority Report. *How to spell Naija, in 100 short stories*, Vol. 2. Gwandustan.

Nwonwu, C. F., 2013a. Annihilation. *Lagos_2060: exciting sci-fi stories from Nigeria*. DADA books.

Nwonwu, M., 2013b. Deletion. *Saraba Online Magazine* [online]. Available at: <http://www.sarabamag.com/deletion/> [Accessed 30 November 2017].

0kogu, E., 2012. Proposition 23. *AfroSF: Science Fiction by African Writers* ed. by I. Hartmann. A StoryTime Publication.

0kogu, E., 2015. An Indigo Song for Paradise. *AfroSFv2* ed. by I. Hartmann. A StoryTime Publication.

Okorafor, N., 2014. *Lagoon*, Hodder & Stoughton.

Okorafor, N., 2015. *The Book of Phoenix*, Hodder & Stoughton.

Olofinlua, T., 2013. Metal Feet. *Lagos_2060: exciting sci-fi stories from Nigeria*. DADA books.

Olukotun, D., 2014. *Nigerians in Space*, Unnamed Press.

Omelsky, M., 2013. African science fiction makes a comeback: A review of Afro SF. *Brittle Paper* [online]. Available at: <http://brittlepaper.com/2013/06/african-science-fiction-comeback-review-afrosf-matt-omelsky/> [Accessed 30 November 2017].

Omelsky, M., 2014. After the End Times: PostCrisis African Science Fiction. *The Cambridge Journal of Postcolonial Literary Inquiry*, 1: 33-49. [online] Available at <https://www.academia.edu/6293082/_After_the_End_Times_Postcrisis_African_Science_Fiction> [Accessed 30 November 2017].

Onwualu, C., 2015. CJ. *Terra Incognita: new short speculative stories from Africa* ed. by N. Dorman. Short Story Day Africa.

Roberts, A., 2005. *The history of science fiction*. Palgrave.

Thompson, T., 2012. Notes from Gethsemane. *AfroSF: Science Fiction by African Writers* ed. by I. Hartmann. A StoryTime Publication.

Thompson, T., 2014. *Bicycle Girl*. Upper Rubber Boot Books.

Thompson, T., 2016a. Budo. Escaped Pod [online podcast]. Available at: <http://escapepod.org/2016/01/20/ep517-budo/> [Accessed 30 November 2017].

Thompson, T., 2016b. *Rosewater*, Apex.

Udo, U. B., 2012. The foreigner. *AfroSF: Science Fiction by African Writers* ed. by I. Hartmann. A StoryTime Publication.

Portrayals of South Africans in Popular Entertainment: Bad Accented Baddies, Prawns and Black Panther

By Robert S. Malan

A lot has happened in a relatively short period for South Africa, since it became a Republic in 1961, independent from British rule. It has been especially interesting to note the changing perception of South Africans in popular entertainment, from the lows of international sanctions as a consequence of apartheid, to when this shameful period was officially ended, by way of Nelson Mandela's release in 1990 and election as President in 1994. Even after this, however, portrayals tended to be a little one-note.

The purpose of this paper is to examine these depictions of South Africans internationally during the apartheid years, and how this evolved in the wake of the science fiction movie District 9[1] and its follow-up, Chappie[2]. Expanding on from that, we'll examine how illustrative these movies were of South Africa as a multi-racial country and, beyond that, representations of Africans in the wider entertainment industry. For this, we'll look at how the recent Black Panther[3] movie marks a breakthrough moment for Africa.

"Diplomatic Immunity"

The year is 1989, and Lethal Weapon 2[4] has just been released.

---

1. *District 9*, 2009. [film] Directed by Neill Blomkamp. South Africa/USA/New Zealand/Canada: TriStar Pictures.
2. *Chappie*, 2015. [film] Directed by Neill Blomkamp. South Africa/USA: Columbia Pictures.
3. *Black Panther*, 2018. [film] Directed by Ryan Coogler. USA: Marvel
4. *Lethal Weapon 2*, 1989. [film] Directed by Richard Donner. USA: Warner Bros.

The first in the series was a major blockbuster hit[5], so a sequel was perhaps inevitable. The plot revolves around the series' lead characters, Martin Riggs and Roger Murtaugh (as played by Mel Gibson and Danny Glover), taking down a group of South African diplomats, who are using their immunity to smuggle gold Kruger Rands.

It's perfectly understandable that white South Africans were fair game for negative portrayals such as this at the time. What is also noticeable were the broad strokes administered to the villains' accents and pantomime-esque portrayals. As Mark Oakley of *Den of Geek* accurately put it, speaking of the actor Joss Ackland's lead antagonist, Arjen Rudd, and his henchmen: "… it's astounding to hear just how poor his accent is on screen … there are countless examples of dreadful accents on show in *Lethal Weapon 2*, mainly from the associated henchmen that make up the bad guys of the piece."[6]

South Africans weren't alone in these types of fast-and-loose portrayals, though. Big budget action films of the eighties were synonymous with cardboard-cut-out non-American characters, in particular Russians and Germans; the movies *Red Heat*[7] and *Die Hard*[8] being particularly prominent examples of this.

Of course, stereotypes such as these were largely shaped by

---

5. The film grossed approximately $120,207,127 worldwide. *IMDb*. [online] Available at: <http://www.imdb.com/title/tt0093409/?ref_=nv_sr_2> [Accessed 15 February 2018].
6. Oakley, M., 2010. *Den of Geek*. [online] Available through: <http://www.denofgeek.com/movies/lethal-weapon/16645/looking-back-at-lethal-weapon-2> [Accessed 15 February 2018].
7. *Red Heat*, 1988. [film] Directed by Walter Hill. USA: Carolco Pictures, Lone Wolf, Oak Pictures.
8. *Die Hard*, 1988. [film] Directed by John McTiernan. USA: Twentieth Century Fox.

news media. In particular, the most prominent white South Africans presented to the world in the media tended to be from the ruling National Party politicians of the time, and other infamous white-supremacy groups like the AWB, as led by Eugene Terreblanche. What they had in common (beyond racist ideals) was a commitment to Afrikaner Nationalism. Afrikaners are mainly descendants of Dutch settlers so, as such, aren't native English speakers. In fact, animosity lingered for many years between Afrikaans and English speaking South Africans; an after-effect of the Boer War, where Boer (ie: Afrikaans-speaking) settlers endured years of struggle against the colonial British Empire.

It's important at this point to clarify that in no way should this be taken as an Afrikaner equals racist statement. As with anything else, some were and others weren't. There are many examples of prominent Afrikaners who opposed and spoke out against apartheid. Pertinent to this paper, and the apartheid era, however, is that many of those who were at the forefront of the regime at the time were Afrikaner nationalists and, so, not native English speakers.

As a result, the "talking heads" acting as representatives of this tended to have distinctive accents and, as such, it is no small wonder that worldwide it became synonymous with white South Africans.

At the same time, portrayals in movies of black South Africans were not particularly nuanced, and inevitably fell prey to non-African stars in leading roles. A case in point is *Cry Freedom*[9], which tells the story of Steve Biko, a black South African activist killed in police custody, as portrayed by

---

9. *Cry Freedom*, 1987. [film] Directed by Richard Attenborough. South Africa/USA: Miramax.

American actor Denzel Washington.

There was a subtle shift after the release of Nelson Mandela in 1990 and the official end of apartheid in 1991. When South Africa won the rugby world cup for the first time in 1995, the country was riding a wave of hope and optimism. This sporting triumph would later be rendered to screen by Clint Eastwood in the 2009 film, *Invictus*[10]. Significantly, however, the lead roles of Nelson Mandela and South African captain Francois Pienaar were taken by Morgan Freeman and Matt Damon respectively – both American.

South Africans were beginning to be accepted into the international entertainment community though, with actors such as Arnold Vosloo and Charlize Theron forging successful careers. Vosloo gained recognition for his role as Imhotep in the 1999 fantasy-adventure film, *The Mummy*[11] and would go on to prominent roles in the likes of the hit US TV show, *Bones*[12], and the 2006 film, *Blood Diamond*[13].

Theron's success was even greater. She was the first South African (and, in fact, African) to win an acting Oscar for her portrayal of serial killer Aileen Wuornos in *Monster*[14] and has become one of the most bankable female actors in Hollywood, starring in the likes of *The Life and Death of Peter Sellers*[15], *Mad*

---

10. *Invictus*, 2009. [film] Directed by Clint Eastwood. USA: Warner Bros.
11. *The Mummy*, 1999. [film] Directed by Stephen Sommers. USA: Universal Pictures, Alphaville Films.
12. *Bones*, 2005 – 2017. [TV] Creator: Hart Hanson. USA: 20th Century Fox Television, Far Field Productions, Josephson Entertainment
13. *Blood Diamond*, 2006. [film]: Directed by Edward Zwick. USA: Warner Bros.
14. *Monster*, 2003. [film]: Directed by Patty Jenkins. USA: Media 8 Entertainment.
15. *The Life and Death of Peter Sellers*, 2004. [film]: Directed by Stephen Hopkins. USA/UK: HBO Films, BBC Films

Max: Fury Road[16], and *Atomic Blonde*[17].

Films also started to present more interesting South African characters, in movies such as *Stander*[18], about the real-life cop-turned-robber, Andre Stander, and *Blood Diamond*. Of course, Leonardo DiCaprio's lead character in Blood Diamond, Danny Archer, is Southern African rather than directly from South Africa, as he is from Zimbabwe (or Rhodesia, as he still calls it); however, his accent is clearly styled on the perceived white South African accent, and some of the words and slang he uses are drawn from Afrikaans.

Blood Diamond is notable for the presence and performance of another actor: Djimon Hounsou, who plays Solomon Vandy, a man who, in his efforts to rescue his son, who has been kidnapped by local rebel militia, is roped into helping Archer. Nominated for an Academy Award, Hounsou is a rare example of a black African actor (he is from Benin, in West Africa) making the breakthrough into Hollywood without having to overtly "Americanise" himself, starring in movies such as *Blood Diamond*, *In America*[19], *The Island*[20], *Gladiator*[21] and *Guardians of the Galaxy*[22].

---

16. *Mad Max: Fury Road*, 2015. [film] Directed by George Miller. Australia/USA: Warner Bros., Village Roadshow Pictures.
17. *Atomic Blonde*, 2017. [film] Directed by David Leitch. Germany/Sweden/USA: 87Eleven.
18. *Stander*, 2003. [film] Directed by Bronwen Hughes. Canada/Germany/South Africa/UK: ApolloProMedia GmbH & Co.
19. *In America*, 2002. [film] Directed by Jim Sheridan. Ireland/UK/USA: Hell's Kitchen Films, East of Harlem (UK) Ltd, Irish Film Industry.
20. *The Island*, 2005. [film] Directed by Michael Bay. USA: DreamWorks, Warner Bros.
21. *Gladiator*, 2000. [film] Directed by Ridley Scott. USA/UK: DreamWorks, Universal Pictures.
22. *Guardians of the Galaxy*, 2014. [film] Directed by James Gunn. USA: Marvel Studios.

Of course, the likes of Stander and Blood Diamond are also some of the many examples of non-South African actors impersonating the accent and thereby compounding existing stereotypes. But then, along came District 9.

Prawns and Tsotsis

South African director Neill Blomkamp was an unknown at the time, but he had a powerful ally in his corner: Peter Jackson, who had become something of a behemoth in Hollywood, thanks to the success of his film adaptation of *The Lord of the Rings*[23]. Blomkamp had been set to direct a Jackson-produced big screen adaptation of *Halo*[24], which fell through. However, so great was Jackson's belief in Blomkamp that he agreed to produce *District 9*, a feature length expansion of the South African's own science fiction short, *Alive in Joburg*[25].

The film is set in an alternate history version of Johannesburg, in 1982 – during the apartheid years. It focuses on the aftermath of an alien ship appearing over the city and becoming stranded. The insect-like aliens are forced to live in a containment camp called *District 9*, bringing them into conflict with the local black township community. As you can guess, the movie is ripe with subtext in its allusions to apartheid, xenophobia, and racial segregation. The aliens are greeted with disgust from all corners and dubbed "Prawns", on account of their physical appearance.

---

23. *The Lord of the Rings: The Fellowship of the Ring* (2001), *The Two Towers* (2002), *The Return of the King* (2003). [film] Directed by Peter Jackson. USA/New Zealand: New Line Cinema, WingNut Films.
24. *Halo*, 2001 – present. [video game series]. USA: Gearbox Software, Bungie Software.
25. *Alive in Joburg*, 2005. [short] Directed by Neill Blomkamp. Canada: Spy Films.

The movie was a critical and financial success[26]. Imaginative in the way it toys with familiar science fiction tropes, turning the ever popular alien invasion plot on its head and throwing it into a unique setting. It was remarkable too for its high production values and, even more crucially, using an unknown South African actor, Sharlto Copley, in the lead role of Wikus van der Merwe. It gave audiences something completely unexpected, and catapulted the South African accent (or at least, the Afrikaans-infused version of it) into the public psyche. It also helped propel Copley to stardom, and he went on to movies like *The A-Team*[27], *Elysium*[28] and *Chappie*.

In the wake of *District 9*'s success, South African accents started to increasingly feature in popular entertainment. There were the aforementioned movies *Elysium*, *Chappie* and *Invictus*, along with *Message from the King*[29], starring pre-*Black Panther* Chadwick Boseman. This upsurge in popularity even filtered into video games. The highest profile of these was *Uncharted 4: A Thief's End*[30], which featured South African accents aplenty, including one of the main characters, Nadine Ross. We'll come back to this particular game and character.

While *District 9* had certainly popularised South Africans, there was still a tendency to cast foreign actors doing impressions of its citizens. Chadwick Boseman plays one in *Message from the King*, though he is American. The British actor Andy Serkis (who had risen to fame on the back of his ground-

---

26. Metascore average rating 81% as at 18/03/2018. Worldwide gross $210,819,611. Figures as per IMDb, 18/03/2018. Available through: < https://www.imdb.com/title/tt1136608/?ref_=fn_al_tt_1> [Accessed 18 March 2018].
27. *The A-Team*, 2010. [film] Directed by Joe Carnahan. USA: 20th Century Fox.
28. *Elysium*, 2013. [film] Directed by Neill Blomkamp. USA: TriStar Pictures.
29. *Message from the King*, 2016. [film] Directed by Fabrice du Welz.
30. *Uncharted 4: A Thief's End*, 2016. [video game]. USA: Naughty Dog

breaking motion-capture performance as Gollum in *The Lord of the Rings*), trotted out a strong faux-Afrikaans accent for his role as Ulysses Klaue, a black market arms dealer, in the Marvel films *Avengers: Age of Ultron*[31] and *Black Panther*. As previously mentioned, *Invictus* featured Americans in the lead roles.

Returning to the character of Nadine Ross in *Uncharted 4* (and its spin-off story, *Uncharted: The Lost Legacy*[32]) we encounter an issue. While the franchise took an important step forward in adding a strong, black woman into the mix, Ross is played by Laura Bailey, a white American. Though there's no doubting Bailey's credentials as a vastly experienced video game voice actor, it still highlights a bigger, recurring problem. At a time when calls for equal representation in entertainment are growing ever louder, this must go down as a baffling decision by game producers Naughty Dog. Surely this was a perfect moment to cast a black South African (or, at the very least, African) in the role. What could have been a resounding statement to their peers instead serves as yet another glaring example of blockbuster entertainment's tone-deaf approach to other cultures and their representations of them.

This brings us back to *District 9*. While it certainly highlighted that there was more to South Africa than apartheid and its inherent struggles it also, along with Blomkamp's next South African-set movie, *Chappie*, suffers from a lack of true representation. Indeed, the central casts in both movies are almost exclusively white. More than this, there are few, if any, sympathetic black characters in either movie. Nigerians

---

31. *Avengers: Age of Ultron*, 2015. [film] Directed by Joss Whedon. USA: Marvel Studios, Walt Disney Pictures.
32. *Uncharted: The Lost Legacy*, 2017. [video game]. USA: Naughty Dog.

suffer the most in this regard, as they are portrayed as ruthless, blood-thirsty traffickers, cannibals, prostitutes, etc. in *District 9*. While it's true that many of the characters in the movie are unsympathetic and exploitative in their own ways, one has to wonder about the omission of black South Africans from the main casts, particularly given the setting and history. It is also begs the question of why Nigerians were so negatively construed, especially as South Africa was (and still is) suffering from post-apartheid xenophobia issues, with Nigerian and Zimbabwean communities in particular often at loggerheads with local South Africans.

One need only look at another South African director in Gavin Hood, and his breakthrough movie, *Tsotsi*[33], by way of comparison. It was the movie that catapulted him to bigger budget, higher profile directing jobs such as *X-Men Origins: Wolverine*[34] and *Ender's Game*[35].

The word "tsotsi"[36] is a South African slang term. It's difficult to fully translate the context behind it without the advantage of having lived in South Africa, but it loosely means "thug" or "criminal". Like *District 9*, the movie is also set in Johannesburg, with large chunks taking place within a local township. The crucial difference with *Tsotsi*, though, is that it is told from the perspective of a young black man, and casts an almost exclusively black local cast, many of whom

---

33. *Tsotsi*, 2005. [film] Directed by Gavin Hood. UK/South Africa: The UK Film & TV Production Company.
34. *X-Men Origins: Wolverine*, 2009. [film] Directed by Gavin Hood. USA/UK: Twentieth Century Fox.
35. *Ender's Game*, 2013. [film] Directed by Gavin Hood. USA: Summit Entertainment.
36. The Collins Dictionary perhaps provides the closest translation, albeit not a perfect one: "a black street thug or gang member". *Collins Dictionary*. [online] Available through: <https://www.collinsdictionary.com/dictionary/english/tsotsi> [Accessed 21 March 2018].

grew up in apartheid-era South Africa, living in townships. Car hijackings and violent theft have long been major issues in latter day South Africa[37], so a movie of this kind, as seen through the eyes of characters who are, on the face of it, largely unsympathetic, was arguably a bold move.

Though *Tsotsi* was a critical success, winning the 2006 Academy Award for Best Foreign Language Film, it didn't have the same impact commercially[38] as *District 9* later would. Of course, you may wonder at the value of comparing two very different sorts of movies, from different genres. There are several interesting and relevant parallels, however. As previously mentioned, both are set in Johannesburg, using townships as their primary locales. Both also hark indirectly to apartheid. However, *Tsotsi* does so far more effectively, daring to show both the ugly and beautiful sides of the country, and posing the question, are even the worst of us beyond redemption? *District 9*, for all its qualities, marginalises and casts a negative light on the many black Africans who were (and still are) forced to live in squalid settlements. It's negligence in this sense is all the more disappointing, given its international success.

As touched upon before, *Chappie*, too, suffers from similar problems. Of the few black members of its cast, they are largely gang members, and its leading cast is almost exclusively white (the one exception being Dev Patel, a British actor of Gujarati Indian descent).

---

37. For the year 01/04/2016 to 31/03/2017 there was a recorded total of 19,016 cases of murder and 16,717 car hijackings. *Africa Check*. [online] Available through: <https://africacheck.org/factsheets/south-africas-crime-statistics-201617/> [Accessed 21 March 2018].

38. A reported worldwide gross taking of $11,054,000 compared to *District 9*'s $210,819,611. *Wikipedia*. [online] Available through: https://en.wikipedia.org/wiki/Tsotsi#Box_office, and https://en.wikipedia.org/wiki/District_9#Box_office> [Accessed 21 March 2018].

This is not a problem that's limited to *District 9* and *Chappie*, of course. Big budget entertainment has a tendency to be somewhat one-note in its depictions of Africa. Too often, the continent is used as a war-ravaged backdrop, with its inhabitants either victims needing to be saved, or fully culpable in the turmoil unfolding around them: helpless victims or cold-hearted killers. That is not to say that movies of this nature are invalid, though. *Blood Diamond*, in amongst its bang and bustle, highlights the darker reality behind the jewellery trade; movies like *Beasts of No Nation*[39], *Hotel Rwanda*[40] and *The Last King of Scotland*[41] are about genuine issues and real-life tragedies. The problem is that this is too often the only facet of Africa portrayed to a worldwide audience.

The *Black Panther* Effect

So, how refreshing to finally have a movie like *Black Panther*. Indeed, it is a game-changer in a number of ways. A big budget production featuring a predominantly black cast is monumental in itself; presenting a new and fresh vision of African culture perhaps even more so. Wakanda, the central (fictional) country, is an exciting concept of an advanced African country. It presents us with a picture of Africans at the forefront of technology, driving its own progression, rather than looking for foreigners from supposedly more "civilised" countries to do so for them.

---

39. *Beasts of No Nation*, 2015. [film] Directed by Cary Joji Fukunaga. USA: Netflix.
40. *Hotel Rwanda*, 2004. [film] Directed by Terry George. UK/South Africa/Italy: United Artists.
41. *The Last King of Scotland*, 2006. [film] Directed by Kevin Macdonald. UK/Germany: Fox Searchlight Pictures.

It even manages to craftily include a scene that acts both as homage and commentary for the James Bond franchise: a casino fight followed by a car chase. The casino itself is a direct nod to a similar setting in the Bond movie, *Skyfall*[42], and then there's the car chase following this, which features an Aston Martin at the heart of the action (Aston Martin, of course, has long been a recurring car choice for the Bond movies).

At a time when there has been much debate and demand for casting a non-white Bond, *Black Panther* managed to sneak in its very own version, as if to say, "What's all the fuss about?". It's just one of the many ways that the movie acts as something of a call-to-action for Hollywood.

Naturally, there are areas where even *Black Panther* might have done more. While its central characters are African, many of the principal players aren't: Chadwick Boseman (T'Challa/Black Panther), Michael B. Jordan (Erik Killmonger), Danai Gurira (Okoye), Sterling K. Brown (N'Jobu), Forest Whitaker (Zuri) and Angela Bassett (Ramonda) are all American, as is writer/director Ryan Coogler and co-writer Joe Robert Cole, while Daniel Kaluuya (W'Kabi) and Andy Serkis (Ulysses Klaue) are British, Letitia Wright (Shuri) is British-Guyanese, Winston Duke (M'Baku) is from Trinidad and Tobago, and Florence Kasumba (Ayo) is German. That said, Kasumba was born in Uganda, Lupita Nyong'o's (Nakia) parents are Kenyan, and she was raised in the country (having been born in Mexico); Daniel Kaluuya is the son of Ugandan immigrants, and Danai Gurira's parents are Zimbabwean. It's good also to see legendary South African actors John Kani (as T'Challa's father, T'Chaka) and David S. Lee (Limbani) in the cast.

---

42. *Skyfall*, 2012. [film] Directed by Sam Mendes. UK/USA: Eon Productions, Metro-Goldwyn-Mayer, Columbia Pictures, United Artists, B23.

It may seem churlish to highlight such things, but how important a step would it be for African actors and creators to be taking centre stage in portrayals of the continent, its people and diverse cultures? While *Black Panther* marks an important stepping stone, forcing open a door that has been closed for far too long, we can be hopeful that the next phase in this evolution will be to see Africans at the forefront of how they are represented, and given the largest possible canvas on which to do so.

Biographies

Ezeiyoke Chukwunonso - Nigeria. MA graduate of Creative Writing, Swansea University Wales. A collection of his stories, *The Haunted Grave and Other Stories* has been published by Parallel Universe Publications. His short stories have appeared in different anthologies around the world.

Polina Levontin - Russia. Scientist. Deals with interdisciplinary research projects, requiring a sufficient understanding of various fields in order to collaborate with ecologists, statisticians, economists, anthropologists and graphic designers. The main theme of her research has been uncertainty in scientific advice. The subject of uncertainty bridges mathematics and storytelling - people rely not just on numbers but on narratives to react to risks. Studying at the Center for Multidisciplinary and Intercultural Inquiry (CMII, UCL) she focused on how science and risk are represented in popular culture, exploring narratives of environmental disasters, genetic engineering and bio-terror. She is the co-editor of Vector - the critical journal of the British Science Fiction Association (BSFA).

Robert S. Malan - South Africa. Author and editor with a passion for storytelling across all media formats - particularly SF, Fantasy and Dark Fantasy. He has published two books for his graphic novel series 'A Darkness in Mind', with artist John Cockshaw: *Quest & The Sign of the Shining Beast* and *The Prisoner*. *Quest & The Sign of the Shining Beast* has been shortlisted for the NOMMO Awards 2018.

Peter J. Maurits - Netherlands. Postdoctoral fellow at the University of Erlangen-Nurnberg. He holds a PhD in comparative literature from the University of Munich, and an MA in literary studies from Utrecht University. His main research interest lies in the way literary forms migrate and adapt over time and space, particularly during globalization. His current research project centres on African science fiction. Formerly he worked on a Mozambican ghost story.

Nick Wood - Zambia/South Africa. Nick is a Zambian born, South African naturalised clinical psychologist, with over twenty short stories previously published in international venues, including *AfroSF* and *AfroSF 2*, amongst others. He has a YA speculative fiction book published in South Africa entitled *The Stone Chameleon* as well as a debut novel *Azanian Bridges*, which has been shortlisted for four Awards, viz. the Sidewise (Alternative History), Nommos (African), BSFA and John W. Campbell (2016). Nick's follow up to *Azanian Bridges* is *Water Must Fall*, a solar-punk thriller, looking for a home.

www.ingramcontent.com/pod-product-compliance
Lightning Source LLC
Chambersburg PA
CBHW071359080526
44587CB00017B/3135